100s OF IDEAS FOR PRIMARY MATHS

PRIMARY BOOKSHELF

100s OF IDEAS FOR PRIMARY MATHS

A cross-curricular approach

Paul Harling

Hodder & Stoughton
LONDON SYDNEY AUCKLAND TORONTO

First published 1990
© 1990 Paul Harling

British Library Cataloguing in Publication Data

Harling, Paul,
    Ideas for maths: a cross-curricular approach. – (Primary
bookshelf).
    1. Primary schools. Curriculum subjects: Mathematics
    I. Title II. Series
    327.7

    ISBN 0–340– 51920– 7

Typeset by Medcalf Type Ltd, Bicester, Oxon

Printed in Great Britain for the educational publishing division of
Hodder and Stoughton Ltd, Mill Road, Dunton Green, Sevenoaks,
Kent by Thomson Litho Ltd, East Kilbride.

Contents

Preface

For many years primary school teachers have been effectively using cross-curricular approaches to general primary education as the basic style of working. This has been because the aims of this fundamental foundation phase have always been much wider than the mere acquisition of subject knowledge. In attempting to include the aesthetic and creative, physical, human and social, moral and spiritual, and technological aspects, as well as the linguist and literary, mathematical and scientific 'cores' they have been eager to use the techniques of curriculum design and imlementation which cross subject boundaries and emphasise the unity of education rather than its separate strands.

This practice has been recognised in the National Curriculum as a valid, fundamental part of the primary teacher's work. Partly as a means of covering more material efficiently, and partly because it emphasises the reality of the world in which we live, a cross-curricular approach has been emphasised in the Programmes of Study and Attainment Targets, as well as in the non-statutory guidance, in the core curriculum areas of Mathematics, Science and English. It is with this in mind that *100s of Ideas for Primary Maths* has been written. The aim of the book is to help primary teachers to develop and sustain this cross-curricular approach using the core subject of mathematics as the basic area of content and approach.

The book is in two parts. Part One concerns the teacher's planning of work. It provides a rationale for the approach, briefly tracing the formal development of the idea as an aspect of educational policy which has culminated in the emphasis placed on this way of working in the National Curriculum documents. A framework for systematic planning of a cross-curricular approach to topics based on mathematics is developed and explained. The framework offered allows the maximum number of opportunities for the teacher to relate the work to the Programmes of Study and Attainment Targets of the National Curriculum. By this means the Attainment Targets at several levels, and in several subject areas, can be covered in a systematic but straightforward way.

Clearly cross-curricular work is particularly relevant when developing activities leading to achievement within the Mathematics Attainment Targets 1 and 9, concerning the use and application of the subject. These 'process' aspects, as well as the situation with regard to assessment, monitoring and record keeping are explained and discussed and advice is offered as to ways in which children can be observed working and their progress appraised.

Part Two of the book is an 'Ideas Bank', consisting of well over 300 activities for cross-curricular work with primary age children. They have been chosen because they either use mathematics as a tool for clarification and explanation, or because they provide a context from another 'subject' which effectively highlights one or more mathematical concepts or principles.

Where appropriate, examples and diagrams are included to indicate a possible approach, an expected response from the children, or a means of analysis and recording the data or the results achieved. Each activity is directly related to relevant Attainment Targets.

The activities are grouped under topic headings which indicate the broad subject matter. There is, however, no necessity to use all the activities suggested within a topic heading, or to avoid dipping into two or more topic headings at the same time. As long as the range of activities chosen is relevant to the general level of the children's attainment, covers a range of skills, allows for a measure of differentiation to meet individual needs, and has a theme which ties together the various chosen activities, then the choice can be open-ended.

Obviously 300 or so activities does not exhaust the possibilities for forging cross-curricular links between mathematics and other subjects. The best teaching ideas, in terms of both content and process, will always arise from on-going work by interested children led by a skilled and enthusiastic teacher. The purpose of the book has been to provide a range of starting points or triggers for extending children's mathematical experience and, where appropriate, to indicate the content and approaches which would encourage the child to move into the world of applied mathematics at a level relevant to his or her own life.

Part One

1 Why use a cross-curricular approach to primary mathematics?

The short answer to this question is 'because the National Curriculum tells us it is a good idea'. However, such a blunt statement does not do justice to the long-standing belief in the need for a cross-curricular approach to primary mathematics expressed in many 'official' and 'private' published sources. Nor does it acknowledge the recognition by the vast majority of primary school teachers that such an approach to all subjects is a desirable and profitable way of educating young children.

The first rumblings of 'official' concern were voiced in *Primary Education in England: A Survey by HM Inspectors of Schools (DES, 1978)*. Chapter 5 contained the observation that teachers were effective at dealing with the 'basic' mathematical ideas. However, when extension or enrichment was required, or when the mathematical concepts and skills needed to be applied to the broader curriculum, teaching was somewhat less effective.

The year 1978 also saw the setting up of the Committee of Enquiry into the Teaching of Mathematics in Schools, under the chairmanship of W.H. Cockcroft. The committee published its report in 1982 and it is commonly known as *The Cockcroft Report* or *Mathematics Counts*. The Report has this to say about the links between mathematics and other curricular areas:

> The experiences of young children do not come in separate packages with 'subject labels'; as children explore the world around them, mathematical experiences present themselves alongside others. The teacher needs therefore to seek opportunities for drawing mathematical experiences out of a wide range of children's activities. Very many curricular areas give rise to mathematics. Measurement and symmetry arise frequently in art and craft; many patterns have a geometrical basis and designs may need enlarging or reducing. Environmental education makes use of measurement of many kinds and the study of maps introduces ideas of direction, scale and ratio. The pattern of the days of the week, of the calendar and of the recurring annual festivals all have a mathematical basis; for older children historical ideas require understanding of the passage of time, which can be illustrated on a 'time-line' which is analogous to the 'number-line' with which they will already be familiar. A great deal of measurement can also arise in the course of simple cookery, including the calculation of cost; this may not always be straightforward if only part of a packet of ingredients has been used. Many athletic achievements require measurement of distance and time. At the infant stage many stories and rhymes rely for their appeal on the pleasure of counting. (Paragraph 325)

It would be easy to compile a much longer list of areas of the primary curriculum which provide opportunities for the use of mathematical skills; pressure of work in the classroom makes it much less easy for the teacher to make sure that advantage is taken of these opportunities when they arise. When planning the activities of the classroom, and especially any extended topic or project work, it is therefore necessary for the teacher to try to identify at the outset the mathematical possibilities which exist within the work which is planned. Not all of these will necessarily be realised but by planning in this way it becomes easier to make the most of whatever opportunities present themselves and perhaps also, by appropriate discussion, to draw attention to others. (Paragraph 326)

One purpose of this book is to attempt to unravel and extend the content of these paragraphs so that valid cross-curricular topics – using mathematical ideas and skills either as the basis, or as a tool for analysis and description within other subjects – can be undertaken to meet the needs of the National Curriculum.

There was in fact an interesting example of educational cross-fertilization at work in the development of general policies for mathematical education in the late 1970s. In 1979 *Mathematics 5–11: A handbook of suggestions* (DES) was published. This book re-highlighted the criteria used in the 1978 Survey for judging the efficacy of a school's organisation of its mathematics education. They bear an uncanny resemblance to the fundamental tenets of good mathematics education as expounded in The Cockcroft Report.

The 1978 and 1979 documents asked:

Does the organisation of mathematics in the primary school provide opportunities for:

(i) direct teaching of individuals, groups of various sizes and the whole class;

(ii) practical work with appropriate materials in a range of situations;

(iii) children to use mathematics across the curriculum and to see the relevance of mathematics in the different areas of study which mathematics pervades;

(iv) discussion and consolidation of mathematical ideas with individuals, groups and the class;

(v) project work or studies;

(vi) effective remedial work for a variety of ability levels;

(vii) extended experiences for the more able pupils;

(viii) children to reflect on their experience and the kind of thinking they are engaged in, so that they are aware that the activities in which they are involved are mathematical;

(ix) children to learn relevant work skills;

- recording and clear presentation, including understanding of why this is important;
- the use of reference books;
- the use of measuring instruments?

Clearly most of these criteria, in addition to being examples of sound practice, are direct reasons why a cross-curricular approach is essential in the primary school curriculum. It should be noted that the criteria were not plucked from thin air at random but were statements of observed successful styles of working exhibited by working primary school teachers.

This idea of primary mathematics education as an active and relevant part of children's lives, and including a wide range of approaches, was further emphasised in the Cockcroft Report, paragraph 243 which states:

Mathematics teaching at all levels should include opportunities for:

- exposition by the teacher;
- discussion between teacher and pupils and between pupils themselves;
- appropriate practical work;
- consolidation and practice of fundamental skills and routines;
- problem solving, including the application of mathematics to everyday situations;
- investigational work.

This paragraph has become, quite correctly, the basic set of tenets for the general design of the mathematics curriculum, particularly at the primary level.

The principles were further reinforced in the HMI document *Mathematics from 5 to 16* (DES 1985) in which it was suggested that:

. . . it is the responsibility of each individual teacher to ensure that mathematics is used where appropriate opportunities occur. At all levels there should be a positive approach to the wide use of mathematics throughout the curriculum. If mathematics is not seen to be needed or used explicitly in project work and in other subjects within the curriculum them the claim that mathematics is a useful subject must sound rather hollow to the pupils. (Paragraph 3.12)

The companion publication to this, *The Curriculum from 5 to 16* (DES 1985) paragraph 12 states:

The various curricular areas should reinforce and complement each other so that the knowledge, concepts, skills and attitudes developed in one area may be put to use and provide insight in another thus increasing the pupils' understanding, competence and confidence.

The aim is therefore to encourage the effective use of mathematics as a tool in a wide range of activities within both school and everyday life. The belief is that by explicitly relating or combining curriculum areas teachers and children will be deterred from seeing school 'subjects' in a narrow sense. The approach may therefore contribute towards improving the efficiency with which the whole curriculum is delivered.

These strands of thought and research have been brought together in the various documents which describe the National Curriculum in terms of its content and approaches, and which offer some advice about the design and implementation of such a curriculum. Each of the separate subject documents emphasises the importance of at least breaking down the barriers between subjects, and preferably making active efforts to join them and relate their content and approaches.

The document *Report of the Task Group on Assessment and Testing: A Digest for Teachers* (DES 1988) stresses the need for a cross-curricular focus in the development of Standard Assessment Tasks or SATs. On page 8 it states:

Some of them [the profile components] should be common to, or overlap, a number of subjects so that cross-curricular themes can be given emphasis.

In similar ways the documents relating to subjects other than mathematics emphasise comparable ideas and hopes. For example *English for Ages 5 to 11* (DES 1988), paragraph 8.27 points out:

In the primary school the programmes of study for various subjects will interact naturally with each other.

Also the Report of the *Design and Technology Working Group* (DES 1988) suggests in paragraph 1.8 that:

We are dealing with an activity which goes across the curriculum, drawing on and linking with a wide range of subjects.

With regard to science the August 1988 proposals document for the *Science for Ages 5 to 16* (DES) National Curriculum points out in paragraph 2.18:

Children do not see the boundaries between one form of knowledge and another since they are intertwined at this stage.

And in paragraph 8.7:

For younger children the integration of science across the curriculum may well be the preferred way of working.

The need for a cross-curricular approach is made quite explicit in the document *Science: Non-Statutory Guidance to the National Curriculum* (DES 1989), paragraph 2.1, where it states:

The attainment targets for each core subject have been developed to take account of the nature, timing and depth of study in other core subjects. This will enable teachers to take achievement in English and mathematics into account in the planning of scientific activities. There are areas of science which require a pupil to be proficient in certain mathematical skills. Where this is the case, on a 'level-by-level' basis, the mathematical work precedes the scientific work. Scientific work can then provide a useful context in which these mathematical skills can be exercised.

The most important point to note when discussing cross-curricular issues is the fact that probably the most significant link between subjects is the person who is attempting to learn them all – namely the child! In his or her life within and outside school experiences rarely occur in separate, subject definable sections. Instead human exploration of the world finds mathematical and other experiences occurring simultaneously, but often in ways in which one kind of skill or experience is able to be used to explain or improve understanding of others.

It has been unfortunate in some ways that the National Curriculum has necessarily been described in terms of 'areas of learning and experience' or 'subjects', because this has had, and will continue to have, an influence on the ways in which the curriculum is planned. The point is that for the primary curriculum the separate elements called 'areas of learning and experience' or 'subjects' are only a tool for planning and analysis. Therefore, as the document *Mathematics: Non-Statutory Guidance to the National Curriculum* (DES 1989) states in paragraph 1.2:

> Planning under subject headings does not . . . preclude flexibility of delivery across subject boundaries. In mathematics, as in other subjects, schools can look for links between the core and foundation subjects and plan for *efficient use of time* [author's emphasis] through cross-curricular work.

Clearly the potential contribution of mathematics to the development and implementation of the whole primary school curriculum is considerable. As well as the cross-curricular enhancement of understanding already mentioned, such an approach can contribute in many ways to the learning of more general skills of written and verbal communication, observation of patterns, consistencies and inconsistencies, similarities and differences, logical reasoning and problem solving. Without doubt the use of a cross-curricular approach to mathematics should help to develop positive attitudes to mathematics and awareness of its power to describe and explain the world by providing methods and frameworks for analysis and study.

Paragraph 1.7 of *Mathematics: Non-Statutory Guidance to the National Curriculum* effectively sums up the situation by stating:

> The incentives for schools to plan cross-curricular approaches to mathematics are clear:
> - they reflect the real world in which we live;
> - they enable more efficient use of time to be planned for;
> - the contribution of mathematics to other areas of the curriculum can be maximised;
> - working in a variety of contexts helps pupils to learn.

It seems to be clear that the whole of the National Curriculum has been designed with the use of cross-curricular approaches in mind as the desirable way for primary school teachers to 'deliver the goods'. Given a degree of acceptance of this principle the question is now one of finding the means to make it work. Some possible answers to this question form the basis for the rest of this book.

2 Planning for a cross-curricular approach

Introduction

The document *Mathematics: Non-Statutory Guidance to the National Curriculum*, paragraph 2.2, states that:

> In primary schools thought needs to be given to:
> - identifying the opportunities that exist for developing mathematics out of cross-curricular topic work, through, for instance, the pupils' own interests and experiences or the environment and the life of the school;
> - deciding which elements of the programmes of study can be delivered through cross-curricular topic work, and which are better approached through more direct teaching in specific mathematics lessons.

Therefore planning for the use of cross-curricular topic work using a mathematical basis is the process of finding and providing sound and useful opportunities for mathematical work to both enrich, and be enriched by, other areas of the curriculum.

Cross-curricular topic work based on mathematics enables children to use skills already learned, and to perhaps meet new ideas in a meaningful context. It may also motivate the need for the learning of new skills. This cyclical process can be illustrated as shown in Figure 1.

Valid use of a cross-curricular approach to the development of mathematical abilities (and abilities in other 'subjects') requires the teacher to have a very clear picture in mind of the ways in which the various 'subjects' of the National Curriculum are structured. The main problem attached to this is that the various documents, while using a common terminology of 'Profile Components', 'Attainment Targets' and the like, are organised in different ways. Also the 'non-statutory guidance' pages, to a large extent, are each unique in structure and directly related to the perceived needs of teachers in relation to that particular subject.

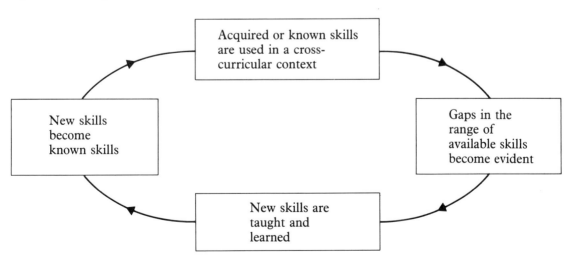

Figure 1 The cycle of acquisition and use of mathematical skills

AT1	Using and applying mathematics	. . . in real life problems and practical tasks . . .
AT2	Number	. . . number notation . . .
AT3	Number	. . . number operations . . . . . . calculations . . .
AT4	Number	. . . estimation and approximation . . .
AT5	Number/ Algebra	. . . patterns, relationships, sequences . . .
AT6	Algebra	. . . functions, formulae equations . . .
AT7	Algebra	. . . graphical representation . . . functions
AT8	Measures	. . . estimation, measurement, approximation . . .

AT9	Using and applying mathematics	. . . in real life problems and practical tasks . . .
AT10	Shape and space	. . . 2 dimensional and 3 dimensional shapes . . .
AT11	Shape and space	. . . location and transformations . . .
AT12	Handling data	. . . collecting, recording, processing data . . .
AT13	Handling data	. . . representing and interpreting data . . .
AT14	Handling data	. . . probability . . .

PROFILE COMPONENT 1 — KNOWLEDGE, SKILLS, UNDERSTANDING AND USE OF NUMBER, ALGEBRA AND MEASURES

PROFILE COMPONENT 2 — KNOWLEDGE, SKILLS, UNDERSTANDING AND USE OF SHAPE AND SPACE AND DATA HANDLING

MATHEMATICS

Figure 2 National Curriculum Core Subjects: Mathematics

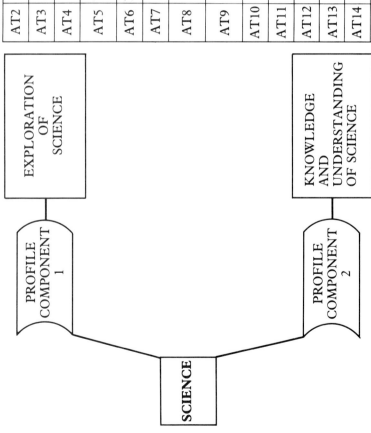

	Exploration of science . . . investigations, hypothesising, exploration . . . sorting grouping, describing, measuring, recording. . . reporting
AT1	

AT2	Variety of life . . . animal and plant life . . .
AT3	Processes of life . . . growth, feeding, movement . . senses
AT4	Genetics and evolution . . . similarities and differences . . .
AT5	Human influences on the Earth . . . environment . . . . . . pollution . . . waste . . decay
AT6	Types and uses of materials . . . similarities and differences . . .
AT7	Making new materials (not applicable to Key Stages 1 and 2)
AT8	Explaining how materials behave (not applicable to Key Stages 1 and 2)
AT9	Earth and atmosphere . . . similarities and differences . . . weather
AT10	Forces
AT11	Electricity and magnetism
AT12	Information technology
AT13	Energy
AT14	Sound and music
AT15	Light
AT16	Earth in space . . . seasons, weather, days, cycles of time
AT17	The nature of science (not applicable to Key Stages 1 and 2)

Figure 3 National Curriculum Core Subjects: Science

9

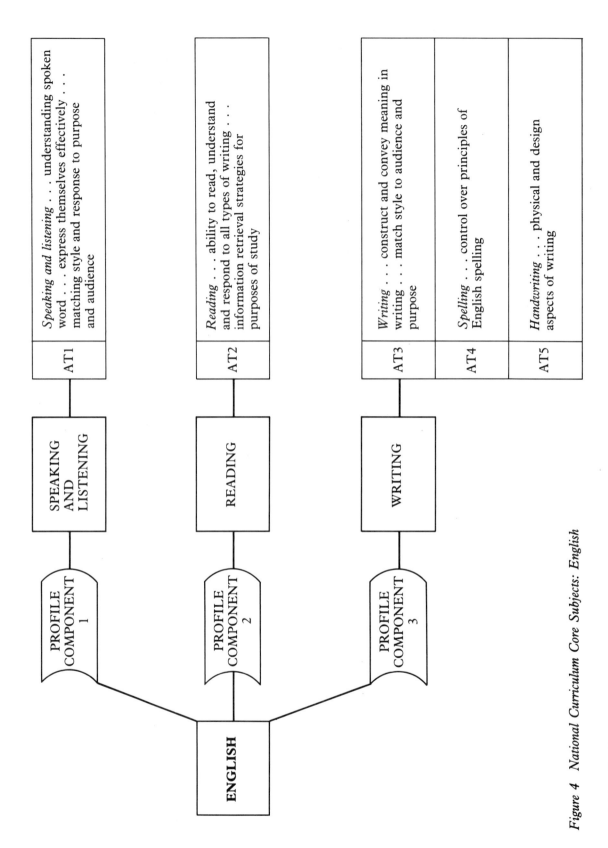

Figure 4   National Curriculum Core Subjects: English

However, it is clear that the three core subjects of the National Curriculum are fundamental to this whole concept of teaching and learning. They form the basis of the Standard Assessment Tasks (SATs) and as 'core' subjects are likely to be evident in almost all cross-curricular work. Therefore some time spent becoming *au fait* with Figures 2, 3 and 4 on pages 8 to 10 of this book will pay good dividends later. It should be noted that they are merely summaries, a means of quickly finding a way around the full documents. No attempt has been made to show all the details of levels within the Attainment Targets. These details are readily available in the National Curriculum documents themselves, which should be constantly available to every teacher.

Assuming a basic familiarity with these, let us move on to the teacher actions necessary to develop a valid cross-curricular topic based on mathematics, using an extended version of a model published by the National Curriculum Council in 1989 (See Figure 5).

Selecting a broad topic

Part 2 of this book offers a range of possible broad topics, aimed at Key Stage 1 and Key Stage 2 of the National Curriculum in Mathematics.

Some aspects can be used in developing work at Level 6, but the main target of the suggested content is the majority of children in primary

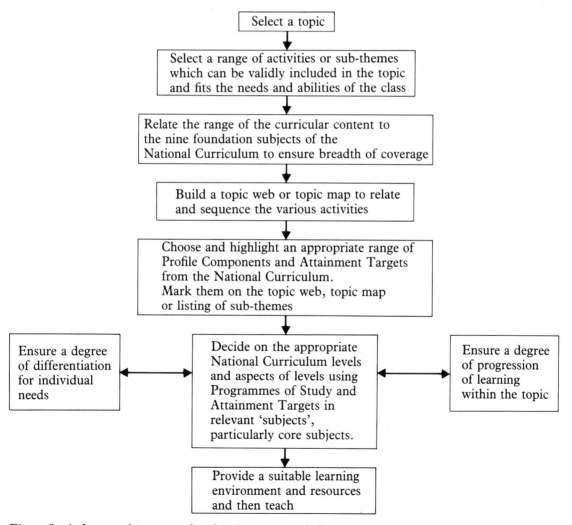

Figure 5 A framework sequence for planning cross-curricular activities

classes. It should be noted that it is not a definitive list, merely a series of suggestions found to be of particular interest to both children and teachers in primary schools. Likewise, the 'titles' are capable of change, combination, and sub-division to suit the needs of the situation. Taken in its entirety the topics include work in most of the nine foundation subjects of the National Curriculum.

Selecting a range of activities or sub-themes

It will always be the case that teacher judgement is required concerning the choice of sub-themes within broad topic headings and so there is no necessity to limit the choice to the suggested ideas in this book. The important point to stress is the need to plan work which will be of interest and benefit to the children in your particular situation and related to on-going work within the whole school curriculum. The intuitive choice of themes will probably provide automatic links between them and, as always, the professional judgement of the teacher will be put to full use in ensuring a cohesive topic possessing continuity, consistency and breadth.

At this stage of planning it would be prudent to make use of an excellent planning device called 'Tetrad Analysis' which was used very effectively in the Open University Course *PME 233 'Mathematics Across The Curriculum'*. This framework encourages a systematic approach to considering the potential and problems associated with teaching using a multi-strand topic. The elements of the tetrad are as follows:

Figure 6   Elements of a Tetrad Analysis

The model highlights the main constituents of any activity – *Goal(s) Tasks Resources* and *Ground*, and also shows the possible interrelationships between the constituent activities.

Look now in turn at the links between each aspect:

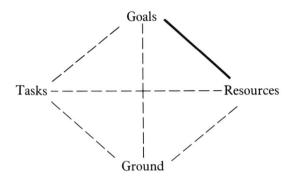

Figure 7   Tetrad Analysis: linking resources and goals

Questions:

■ Do I have the resources (equipment, time, personpower) to achieve the goals of this cross-curricular topic?

■ Which locations, inside and outside the school, do I need access to in order to encourage effective real learning within the other curricular areas included in the topic?

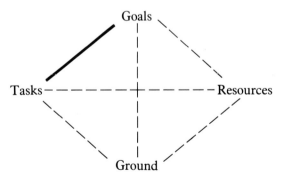

Figure 8   Tetrad Analysis: linking goals to tasks

Questions:

■ Are the tasks I have chosen cohesive and likely to achieve my goals in this topic?

12

- Can a degree of progression be built into the tasks so that all children can achieve the goal(s) set?

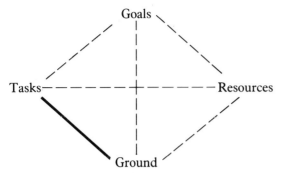

Figure 9   Tetrad Analysis: linking ground to tasks

Questions:

- Do the pupils already possess skills and knowledge necessary to undertake these particular cross-curricular activities?

- Do the tasks/activities give me chances to teach or develop new skills, concepts or abilities?

- Are the tasks/activities of a sufficient range to allow for differentiation taking account of children's different levels of ability and experience?

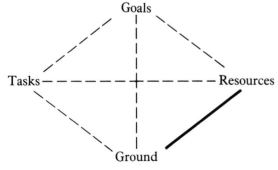

Figure 10   Tetrad Analysis: linking ground to resources

Questions:

- Are the children able to use the equipment available to them?

- What skills may I need to teach in order for children to make full use of equipment?

- What issues of safety and health need to be taken account of or trained for?

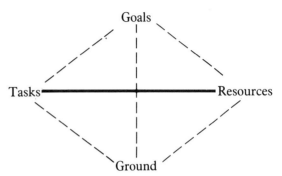

Figure 11   Tetrad Analysis: linking resources to tasks

Question:

- What resources do I actually need to acquire or create for the chosen range of activities?

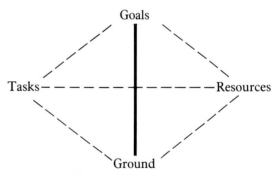

Figure 12   Tetrad Analysis: linking ground to goals

Question:

- Are the pupils actually achieving the goal(s)?

These questions effectively constitute a checklist for ensuring cohesion in cross-curricular topic work and are especially useful if you are developing a topic from a mathematical base.

Relating the proposed range of content to the National Curriculum

This stage of planning provides an opportunity for you to ensure that a sufficient, and justifiable, breadth of curricular coverage is implicitly or explicitly included in the topic.

The nine foundation subjects are:

Mathematics ⎱
English   ⎰ core subjects
Science   ⎰
Technology (including design)
History
Geography
Music
Art
Physical Education

It is clearly not necessary to include all of the 'areas' in every topic. A grid can be drawn up quite easily (see Figure 13) once the desired sub-themes have been chosen and listed, so that the omissions can be remedied and excessive duplication eliminated.

Building a topic web

The use of a topic web or topic map is a well-established device for refining and defining aspects of a broad topic which can be investigated in the classroom. If it is mounted and displayed in a public place in the classroom it can also provide an excellent reference point for groups of children to see how their own 'bit' fits in with the overall topic being covered.

Again, using the broad topic of 'pets' as an example the basic structure might be as shown in Figure 14. From such a structure the sequence and links can be established to suit the particular needs of the teacher, children and geographical situation.

Choosing appropriate Attainment Targets

This is an essential stage in the process since the purpose of the cross-curricular planning is to cover a range of Profile Components and Attainment Targets concurrently. The point of the exercise is to highlight the aspects of the National Curriculum which:

Overall topic: Pets									
Sub themes	Art	History	English	Mathematics	Geography	Physical education	Science	Music	Technology
1 Food and its costs			✓	✓			✓		
2 Homes and accomodation	✓		✓	✓			✓		✓
3 Vets; health		✓	✓	✓	✓		✓		✓
4									
5									

Figure 13   Relating the proposed content to the National Curriculum

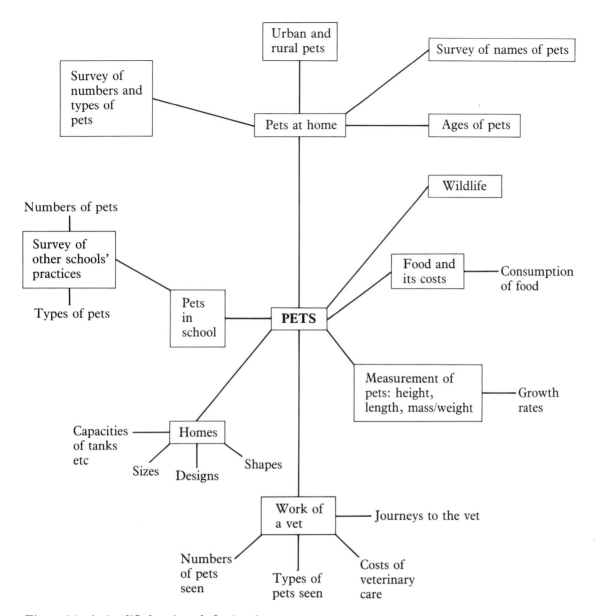

Figure 14 A simplified topic web for 'pets'

1 *are* covered in the topic so that assessments and judgements can be made about children's attainments; and

2 are *not* covered in the topic so that aspects omitted (deliberately or accidentally) can be remedied either by further current planning or by including the aspects in later topics or by specific subject-based teaching.

Such decisions depend on:

(a) the amount of time allocated to cross-curricular activities relative to subject-specific teaching and learning;

(b) the number of topics expected to be completed in a given school year, or sub-phase (Key Stage 1 or Key Stage 2) or in the whole primary phase of education;

(c) the desired scope of the particular topic. If it is a 'small' topic based predominantly on mathematics then it is likely that a smaller range of Attainment Targets in other 'subjects' can be satisfactorily covered. If the time allocation is short, perhaps because the basic stimulus is an event in the school calendar, or a short series of television programmes, or the availability of some items of borrowed equipment or specialist teaching expertise, then the same limitations apply.

Topic: Pets

	PC	AT	Covered fully at required level	Partially covered at required level
Mathematics	1	1		
	1	2		
	1	3		
	1	4		
	1	5		
	1	6		
	1	7		
	1	8		
	2	9		
	2	10		
	2	11		
	2	12		
	2	13		
	2	14		
English	1	1		
	2	2		
	3	3		
	3	4		
	3	5		
Science	1	1		
	2	2		
	2	3		
	2	4		
	2	5		
	2	6		
	2	9		
	2	10		
	2	11		
	2	12		
	2	13		
	2	14		
	2	15		
	2	16		
(Other foundation subjects noted in a similar way)				

Figure 15 Schedule for noting appropriate Attainment Targets and Profile Components

Assuming access to the National Curriculum documents, the associated Profile Components and Attainment Targets can be noted on the topic web itself relating to particular sub-themes or on a separate general grid such as the one shown in Figure 15. It can be used either to scan the whole topic or to scan the sub-themes.

Determining the National Curriculum Levels

Given the previous determination of the broad scope and sequence of the topic, as discussed so far in this chapter, it is essential to ensure that the appropriate National Curriculum 'Levels' are recognised, noted, and adhered to in order that the topic is appropriate for the particular set of children involved. It should be noted, however, that there are levels within the 'Levels' of the National Curriculum. 'Levels' 3 and 4 are particularly full.

The suggestion is that work at two, or at the most three, adjacent levels is encouraged within the designated Profile Components and Attainment Targets, in the design of the detailed tasks for groups and individual children. This would allow you to:

1 have an average target level for the general activities undertaken and the expected responses of children;

2 build in a degree of progression to encourage development of skills, concept understanding and ability to apply ideas;

3 differentiate work set and expected responses from children to take account of individual needs and abilities.

Providing the learning environment and teaching

It is not the purpose of this section to provide yet another psychology-based manual of ideals about ways in which children acquire, or should acquire learning and ways teachers carry out, or should carry out, their functions as teachers. Rather, the purpose is to provide some pointers about general means by which teachers might analyse their roles

in relation to cross-curricular topics in mathematics. The desired role of the child in cross-curricular studies is clearly emphasised in the National Curriculum. Paragraph 5.3 of *Mathematics: Non-Statutory Guidance to the National Curriculum* states that:

> All pupils, from the earliest stages onwards, should be involved increasingly in determining their next targets, and in making decisions about the organisation and pace of their work.

The emphasis in topic work in general, and in cross-curricular mathematics work in particular, is therefore acknowledged to be one of developing the independence of the pupil in relation to learning strategies and the processes of mathematical thinking and actions. Thus it might be advisable for each teacher to examine his or her assumed roles and perhaps ensure that a wider range of roles is adopted to attempt to further develop this sense of personal responsibility desired in children.

There are four broad groupings of 'role' applicable to this sort of work.

1 The Leader

Creator: Produces a learning environment in which children's own ideas are valued.
Stimulator: Encourages children to express their ideas and feel responsible for their actions.
Intermediary: Encourages child to child discussion and interaction rather than teacher to child.
Manager: Organises and supervises general classroom activities.
Presenter: Stimulates initially, offers and gives information and clarifies requirements.

2 The Administrator

Facilitator: Ensures good management of time on-task and between tasks to allow for reflection on work done and work to be done.
Coordinator: Ensures that all children are informed of the work others are doing.
Time Economist: Ensures that children's work is not replicated or lacking progression.
Enabler: Ensures the availability of cross-

curricular facilities in other parts of the school and environment. Smooths the path for children to use people, locations and resources outside the classroom.

3 The Intervener

Adviser: Listens to children and suggests possible alternative approaches.

Observer: Studies the progress and processes used by groups and individual children, giving feedback where necessary.

Challenger: Uses open-ended questions to stimulate the pupils' own thinking.

Critic: Comments critically but in an atmosphere of 'acceptance of criticism' developed using the other roles.

Respondent: Answers direct pupil queries, but in a way which provides information rather than instruction about how to think.

4 The Evaluator

Assessor: Encourages the child to understand that 'measurements' are to be made about the quantity and quality of activity and learning.

Judge: Continually judges progress and acts on the judgement in a formative way.

Any teacher undertaking cross-curricular work in the systematic way which is now required has to 'stand back' occasionally from his or her normal model of teaching and assume one or more different roles. Perhaps some of those listed here are of help in defining either actual or desired action. However, all are necessary at one time or another if effective work is to occur which is not directly initiated and controlled by the teacher. That degree of flexibility in both teachers and children is the essence of a cross-curricular approach.

3 The 'process' factors in cross-curricular mathematics topics

The Attainment Targets set out in the National Curriculum documents represent the knowledge, skills and understanding which would be covered, at different levels appropriate to the child, during the years of schooling. The targets are a means of specifying the breadth of the education to be made available to all children but, in conjunction with the Programmes of Study, they also provide an indication of possible routes or sequences along which the child might be led.

However, there is a major implication leading from the provision of a systematically organised curriculum which possesses such a breadth and progression. For most people the main point of learning a subject is to be able to use it effectively and, hopefully, creatively and with confidence. Unfortunately the ability to 'use' a subject like mathematics in practical, real-world problems is not an innate feature of adults or children. It has to be taught. It is therefore essential to pay attention to the 'process' elements of cross-curricular work as well as to the listings of knowledge and skills. As the August 1988 proposals document for *Mathematics for Ages 5 to 16* (DES) in the National Curriculum points out:

> The ability to apply mathematical skills in *defined and narrow contexts* [author's emphasis] is an essential prerequisite for tackling successfully practical or real-life problems.

These 'defined and narrow contexts' can be based on selections from the topics and sub-themes which are offered in Part 2 of this book, and from which 'structured' training can be offered to all children.

The point is again stressed in *Mathematics: Non-Statutory Guidance to the National Curriculum* paragraph 1.2:

- Gaining knowledge and developing skills and understanding in mathematics facilitates and enables the use and application of mathematics in solving problems.
- Tackling problems, both of the practical, 'real-life' sort, and within mathematics itself, motivates and requires the learning of further skills and the development of greater understanding.

The capacity to use or apply mathematics efficiently and effectively to practical tasks depends on a range of skills and qualities worthy of clear specification so that their existence can be overtly included in any cross-curricular activities.

There are three broad groups of 'skills and qualities' which can be isolated and listed, and which are stated or implied in the National Curriculum documents.

Modes of learning and use of strategies

As specified in the document *Mathematics: Non-Statutory Guidance to the National Curriculum*, the overall scheme of work should include the following, all of which are of direct relevance to cross-curricular work:

Listening: Hearing and understanding explanations, instructions, questions, answers.

Reading: Studying from textbooks or work cards, researching from topic books or reference books; comparing methods or solutions; gaining feedback from the computer monitor.

Writing: Pencil and paper calculations; drawing sketches and diagrams; recording the results of discussions, experiments or surveys; reporting on a project.

Talking: Describing; explaining; clarifying ideas; giving examples; making predictions; asking questions; reporting outcomes; talking through difficulties; discussing with peers.

Reflecting: Considering approaches to problems.

Carrying our practical work: Sorting; counting; measuring; making models; trying out different arrangements; carrying out surveys; writing – and detecting and correcting errors in – a computer program.

Observing: Watching what is happening; spotting patterns; looking for consistencies or inconsistencies; noting similarities or differences.

Drafting: Plotting out the sequence of steps and the layout of a particular assignment.

More specifically the aims are that children should be able to:

- Select whatever mathematics is appropriate for the particular task.
- Apply the mathematics sensibly and efficiently.
- Try alternative strategies if needed.
- Check on progress at appropriate stages.
- Analyse the final results to ensure that the initial requirements have been met.

Still more specifically the objectives are that children should be able to:

- Formulate a plan of what needs to be done, identifying any sub-tasks.
- Decide whether there is enough information – and if not, decide what they need and where to find it.
- Distinguish between important and irrelevant information.
- See how the task is similar to, or differs from, earlier tasks.

- Recognise patterns, relationships or connections and/or general rules.
- Select the appropriate mathematics to create a model.
- Apply commonsense and reasoning skills.
- Select and use the most appropriate technology.
- Recognise that the best 'mathematical' solution may not be the best 'real' solution.
- Complete the task.

Communication skills

Skill in communication of ideas is generally important in life, and in the educational process, but is particularly so in any cross-curricular mathematical work. Group discussion is an essential aspect which can greatly enhance pupil performance, especially if combined with the need to present results, findings, models made and ideas understood to other pupils and adults. Specifically it is suggested in the document *Mathematics: Non-Statutory Guidance to the National Curriculum* that pupils need to:

- Understand what needs to be done in broad terms;
- Follow instructions from the teacher, the text or the computer;
- Discuss difficulties and ask questions;
- Debate possible courses of action with others;
- Use reference material as appropriate;
- Present and explain results to other pupils, teachers and other adults;
- Make a report;
- Discuss the implications and accuracy of the conclusions reached;
- Relate the result to the world about them as appropriate;
- Discuss other possible interpretations of the conclusions.

The other core subjects suggest emphasis on communication skills in a similar way. In particular paragraph 2.3 of the document *Science: Non-Statutory Guidance to the National Curriculum* relates selected statements of attainment (see

LEVEL 4

SCIENCE	MATHEMATICS	ENGLISH
Be able to describe the story of some scientific advance	Record findings systematically and present them in oral, written, diagrammatic form as appropriate	Give a detailed account of an event, or something that has been learned in the classroom
Draw conclusions from experimental results	Select the materials and the mathematics to use for a task: plan methodically	Draw on reading experience to make comparison and note parallels
Describe investigations in the form of ordered prose using a limited technical vocabulary		Organise non-chronological writing in a logical way

LEVEL 5

SCIENCE	MATHEMATICS	ENGLISH
Suggest simple questions for investigation and safely carry out an investigation using them	Select the material and the mathematics to use for a task; check there is sufficient information; work methodically and review progress	Select and use appropriate referencing skills when pursuing an independent line of enquiry
Be able to argue for and against particular planning proposals in the locality which may have an environmental impact	Interpet mathematical information presented in oral, written or diagrammatic form	Contribute and respond constructively in discussion or debate, advocating and justifying a particular point of view

Figure 16 Linking the core subjects in terms of communication skills

Figure 16), using Levels 4 and 5 as the example, in order to highlight the links between the core subjects in terms of communication skills. Of course, the same can be done for each National Curriculum 'Level' if needed for detailed planning of a cross-curricular topic.

Attitudes and personal approaches to work

Effective teaching at all levels and stages has always been concerned with the social and emotional security and development of children. Cross-curricular work in mathematics is no different. In fact the National Curriculum clearly specifies the need to take account of this aspect in all work. Paragraph 5.13 of the document *Mathematics: Non-Statutory Guidance to the National Curriculum* states:

The personal qualities which pupils need to develop include:

■ motivation and preparedness to tackle the unfamiliar and unknown – willingness to 'have a go';
■ flexibility and creative thinking in overcoming difficulties and developing new approaches;

- perseverance, reliability and accuracy in working through a sequence of stages in an extended task;
- willingness to check, monitor and control their own work;
- independence of thought and action as well as the ability to cooperate within a group;

- systematic work habits.

While these are apparently general to all learning they should be clearly borne in mind at all stages of planning and implementation of cross-curricular mathematical activities, and opportunities should be provided for children to practise and develop such aspects of learning.

4 Assessment, monitoring and record keeping

Assessment of progress has always been an important function of the teaching-learning process in all areas of the curriculum. In the development and use of cross-curricular topics based on mathematics the importance of valid and reliable assessment, and associated record keeping techniques, has become paramount.

Assessment is used to inform both child and teacher of individual and collective progress. It can also help the teacher to diagnose the problems (or otherwise) of children and therefore provides a basis for future planning. Assessment is therefore a means to an end. The end is the achievement, by the child, of the aims and objectives of their education, and thus any useful system of assessment must be directly related to those specific purposes.

Assessment is an integral part of the National Curriculum, and a national assessment system has been developed to provide a framework for all assessment activities undertaken by the school.

The purposes are set out in the document *National Curriculum: From Policy To Practice* (DES, 1989), paragraph 6.2 The national assessment system is:

Formative: in providing information which teachers can use in deciding how pupils' learning should be taken forward, and in giving pupils themselves clear and understandable targets and feedback about their achievements. It also provides teachers and others with the means of identifying the need for further diagnostic assessments for particular pupils where appropriate to help their educational development.

Summative: in providing overall evidence of the achievements of a pupil and of what he or she knows, understands and can do.

Evaluative: in that comparative aggregated information about pupils' achievements can be used as an indicator of where there needs to be further effort, resources, changes in the curriculum, etc.

Informative: in helping communication with parents about how their child is doing, and with governing bodies, LEAs and the wider community about the achievements of a school.

Helpful for **Professional development**, in that the process of carrying out systematic assessment, recording attainment, and moderating the outcomes in discussion with other teachers will provide a valuable basis for teachers to evaluate their own work and to gain access to new thinking.

These broad purposes are to be achieved by use of a combination of modes of assessment. In particular two broad types of assessment are used, Standard Assessment Tasks (SATs), which are national standardised tests, and Teachers' (own) Assessments, (TAs), the latter carried out over an extended period. The idea is that the former are 'yardsticks' against which the more rounded qualitative judgements made by teachers can be moderated.

Teachers' (own) Assessments (TAs) take a variety of forms but should include:

1 assessment and recording of pupils' progress against each of the Attainment Targets;
2 use of a variety of methods of assessment, with enough flexibility built in to reflect the teachers' approach to teaching and the particular situation of the school; and
3 most importantly, Teachers' (own) Assessment should incorporate some carefully designed

assessment tasks which are closely related to the cross-curricular structure and style of the SATs at Key Stages 1 and 2. This structuring must be regarded as of especial importance in the years in which children do not need to 'do' the national SATs.

Careful choice and use of the ideas and topics presented in Part 2 of this book provide ample resources for the development of the children's skills and abilities to help them cope with formal SATs as a normal part of school life. This can be part of, or in addition to, the use of such cross-curricular topics as a valid approach to everyday teaching.

The tasks and activities in Part 2 have been designed to take a variety of amounts of time, and vary in scope to allow professional initiative by the teacher while reflecting the structure of the tasks detailed in the National Curriculum. Some of the tasks are suitable for individuals, others for small groups of pupils. It is suggested that the younger pupils need a group-based structure to predominate until they have developed the maturity needed to persevere with a task on their own. Responses are likely to take a variety of forms, including drawings, oral reports, basic computer 'word processing', graphical representation and model-making.

Others are more extensive and open-ended in character and can be arranged to allow pupils to have some control of the direction they take and the methods they use. It is important that children have a say in their work, because it is crucial that children are able to use initiative, planning skills and work skills, all of which are part of Attainment Targets 1 and 9.

Various organisational possibilities are feasible. For example:

1 All groups of pupils in a class might work simultaneously on the same problem and therefore children's output and achievements can be directly compared and related to Programmes of Study, Attainment Targets and the 'process' objectives.

2 The class in collaboration with the teacher, or the teacher alone, might start with one topic or sub-theme and allow different groups to tackle different aspects of it. This requires the teacher to have knowledge of the mathematical content of each aspect so that appropriate judgements can be made in relation to relevant Attainment Targets. The 'process' element can be concentrated on the skills associated with collaboration and group work.

3 Each group of pupils may be asked to select an activity, problem or task from the lists presented in Part 2. This mode of working requires the teacher to keep long-term curricular content records to ensure that, over time, a sound range of skills, processes and knowledge are included, used by the children, and assessed by the teacher.

4 A group of pupils may wish to work on a task they have identified themselves. The teacher can then add this to the range of ideas presented under each topic heading, and offer extensions from the available lists if appropriate. The same proviso as in the previous item applies to the style of working.

The possible range of output of extended tasks could therefore be wide and cover the whole range of means of pupil recording listed in paragraph 4.6 of the document *Mathematics: Non-Statutory Guidance to the National Curriculum*:

- symbolic
- graphical
- diagrammatic
- pictorial
- written
- constructed
- verbal

Given the extensive publication of the purposes, scope and techniques of the National Curriculum assessment system in other documents there is no need to supply yet another model applicable to the same ground in this short book of ideas. However, it should be noted that each school needs to have an agreed policy towards assessment of all children's work, and in particular cross-curricular projects, which matches or reflects the requirements of both the LEA and the national arrangements. In a similar way LEA and national policy has increasingly determined the nature of records of pupils' work and progress and must be taken account of in agreeing school policies with regard to the 'recording' of cross-curricular topics.

Chapters 2 and 3 of this book provided some listings of criteria against which pupil progress can be assessed and from which valid and reliable records can be built and kept, including attainment of content targets, proficiency in the processes of working mathematically, and the development of attitudes. In the final analysis, however, there is no substitute for a teacher planning systematically in order to 'know' the work being done, and by continuous observation 'knowing' the child and his or her work. No amount of formal assessment or record keeping can remove or replace the professional knowledge of the teacher. If the national or local systems of assessment and record keeping are felt to be valid to your particular situation then use them. If not, then supplement them, amend them or edit them to fit the needs of your school. The 'bottom line' is being able to justify and support your judgements of a child's work by your ability to produce 'hard' evidence, if required, to back up your experienced professional opinion. The topics in Part 2 of this book should help you to do just that, especially if planned and executed systematically in relation to the principles set down in the previous pages.

Part Two –
The Ideas Bank

Introduction

This section consists of over 300 activities for cross-curricular work within Key Stages 1 and 2 of the National Curriculum. These activities provide ample opportunities for work which makes direct use of the abilities detailed in Attainment Targets 1 and 9 and in the non-statutory guidance for the mathematics curriculum.

The activities cover a wide range of approaches and starting points. Some use mathematics as a tool for clarification and explanation of phenomena, patterns or the results of surveys of the environment of children. Others make use of contexts more often seen in non-mathematical work to highlight the power and usefulness of mathematics. All cross subject boundaries, and together the activities include work in all the foundation subjects of the National Curriculum. However, the activities are especially relevant to work which links the core subjects of English, mathematics and science. All essentially concern the application of mathematics to 'real-world' situations and are fundamentally based in the child's experience within and beyond school.

It would be possible for you to open Part 2 at any page, and then simply choose and develop an activity at random. However, this would be likely to lead to fragmentation of the curriculum and a sense that the activity is an end in itself rather than a means to an end. You are therefore strongly advised to use the simple planning model developed and explained in Part 1. In particular, Chapter 2 is concerned with 'planning for a cross-curricular approach' and includes advice about ways topics and activities can be chosen and developed so that they make a direct contribution to the development of the children. This is particularly important within the framework of the National Curriculum. Attention is especially drawn to the framework/sequence shown on page **00** and the subsequent explanatory pages which use the topic of pets as an example.

One final point is worthy of note. Emphasis on 'Use and Application' of mathematics is cross-curricular contexts is a fundamental tenet of the National Curriculum. The techniques which children employ constitute the 'process' objectives of mathematics. Therefore it must be regarded as essential that you are familiar with these aspects. They have been summarised in Chapter 3 and could form a basis for observation of how well children are able to work as a complement to the more usual observation of what they have learned.

Successful implementation of the National Curriculum is basically about teacher awareness of the range and sequence of activities coupled with professional common sense. Much of the desired range and sequence forms the substance of this book. Common sense is already part of your armoury of professional skills.

Book Club

- Using a commercial book club sales pamphlet a good deal of simple data can be gathered and analysed, or mathematical questions asked and answered. Given the books available for a particular term, such problems as the following put 'budgeting' into a real context:

  If a child had £5 to spend, find the possible sets of books which could be purchased from the club with a total cost of less than £5, but giving less than 50p in change.
  ATs 1,2,3

- Survey the costs of the books available for the term. Produce a *histogram* of the data, using the numbers of books on the vertical axis and the costs as a *continuous* variable on the horizontal axis.
  ATs 9, 12, 13

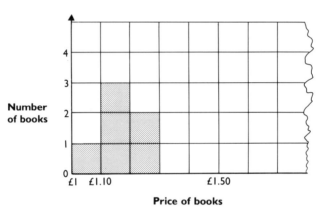

Price of books

- List the available 'books of the term' in order of cost. List the books in order of the number of pages. Make a scattergraph to see if there is any relationship between the two sets of data.
  ATs 1, 2, 3, 9, 13

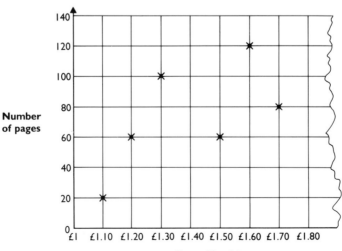

Cost of book

Bridges

- Fold an A4 sheet of thin card into two halves. Investigate the number of exercise books of identical size that can be supported by the card standing on its 'end'.

The activity can be extended to allow different ways of folding the sheet of card. Different ways of folding will support different numbers of books. Possible types of structure are:

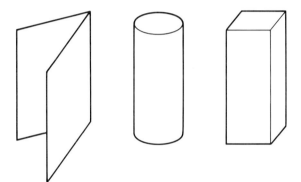

The data should be recorded on a chart and graphed in an appropriate way.
ATs 1, 8, 9, 10, 12, 13

For example:

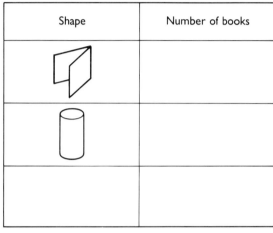

Shape	Number of books

- Create a 10 cm gap between two tables. Use A4 thin card to create a series of 'bridges' to span the gap. Investigate the 'weight' which the structures will hold before collapsing into the gap. Record in a table and by pictorial or graphical means.
ATs 1, 8, 9, 10, 12, 13

- Extend the exercise to other kinds of bridges, including a suspension bridge. A good reference book is *Bridges and How They are Built*, by D. Goldwater, published by World's Work.
ATs 1, 8, 9, 10, 12, 13

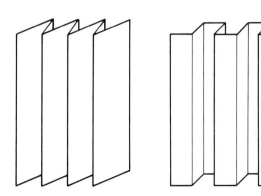

Building site

- Tally and record the numbers of men and women working on a local building site. Some interesting social comment can ensue!
  ATs 1, 2, 3, 9, 12, 13

	Tally	Total
Men	ⅢⅠ ⅢⅠ ⅢⅠ ⅢⅠ ⅢⅠ ⅢⅠ ⅢⅠ ⅢⅠ	
Women	ⅠⅠ	

- Tally and record the number of machines on the site, sorted under suitable headings, for example cranes, diggers, transporters, mixers and so on.
  ATs 1, 2, 3, 9, 12

- Examine and sketch ways in which materials are stacked. For example, pipes are likely to be stacked in this way:

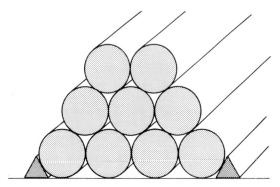

  A model can be made using toilet roll centres.
  ATs 1, 5, 8, 9, 10, 11

- Tally and record the range of hand tools used on the site. Count and record the numbers of shovels, picks, mechanical drills and so on. These can be sorted into sets, and sub-sets, and recorded using Venn diagrams or Carroll diagrams.
  ATs 1, 2, 3, 9, 12

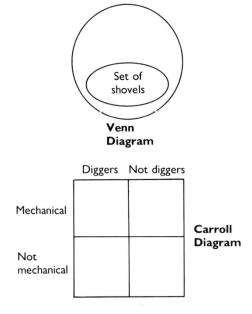

Venn Diagram

Carroll Diagram

- Observe and record examples of known three-dimensional shapes found on the site, for example cylinders, cuboids, triangular prisms.
  ATs 9, 10

- Observe and record patterns in finished or part-finished brickwork or tiling.
  ATs 10, 11, 12

- Use plumb lines and spirit levels to test items in the classroom to see if they are vertical or horizontal.
  ATs 9, 11

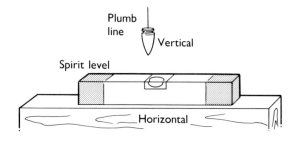

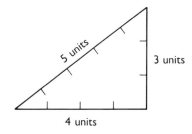

5 units

3 units

4 units

- A rope of 12 units in length can be knotted at intervals of 3 units, 4 units and 5 units. When the rope is 'stretched' holding the knots, a right angle is produced and can be used to check the accuracy of corners of brickwork or paths.
ATs 9, 10

- Estimate and, if possible, measure the dimensions of the site using a trundle wheel and a 20 m surveyor's tape measure. Stress the approximate nature of all measurements but also the need for a degree of accuracy in, for example, building a wall in a straight line.
ATs 1, 8, 9, 11

- Make a plan of the site, first by informal sketching of the location of the parts. It is probable that an outline site plan can be acquired from the contractor for comparison.
ATs 1, 8, 9, 11

- Discuss and decide upon a means of precisely identifying the location of any point on the site – perhaps by the drawing of a grid on which *coordinates* and *addresses* can be specified by an 'ordered pair' of numbers.
ATs 9, 11

- Draw sketches of plans, front elevations and side elevations of one or more of the buildings. The architect of the site may be able to offer an actual set of plans for comparison.
ATs 1, 8, 9, 10, 11

- Survey and analyse in an *attribute matrix* the different ways in which items are transported on a building site.
ATs 1, 9, 12, 13

For example:

	Barrow	Hod	Dumper
Sand	✓		✓
Cement	✓		✓
Bricks	✓	✓	✓

- Investigate the use of 'triangles' to create rigid structures in scaffolding or in the arm of a crane. The investigation can be done using geostrips and fasteners or straws and pipe cleaners.
ATs 9, 10, 11

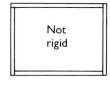

Not rigid

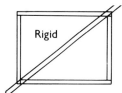

Rigid

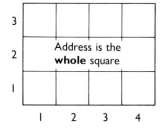

Address is the **whole** square

Coordinates are found at the intersection of the lines

Cars

- Survey the makes or models of cars passing the gates of the school. Tally the data and produce a graphical representation of the results. Check in a newspaper the current sales figures for different makes and models of cars. Decide whether the sample passing the school is representative of the numbers of cars manufactured.
  ATs 1, 2, 3, 4, 9, 12, 13

- Survey and find the most frequent colour used on the bodywork of cars.
  ATs 1, 3, 4, 9, 12, 13

- The registration or number plate of most cars indicates the town or city in which the vehicle was first registered by use of a 'coded' pair of letters. Survey traffic on a local, but major road, to try to find the proportion of the cars which are 'local'. (The information can be requested from the local vehicle registration office, the AA or the RAC.)
  ATs 1, 2, 4, 5, 9, 12, 13

- Survey cars in a car park to determine the ages of the vehicles. Despite the existence of some even older vehicles in the staff car park it would be useful to take 1970 as the base year. In that 'motoring year' from 1 August 1969 to 31 July 1970 all newly registered vehicles had a registration number consisting of three letters, up to three numbers and then a final letter H. Trace and define each 'motoring year' up to the current year before commencing the survey. Ignore all personalised number plates. The average age of vehicles in different locations can be ascertained in a similar way.
  ATs 1, 3, 4, 6, 9, 12, 13

- Using staff cars, parents' cars and a variety of car magazines a data base, built on to a computer program or a card index, can be designed and analysed to consider such factors as cost when new, current values, amount on depreciation, top speed, expected fuel consumption, costs to run for a year, whether an object of given size will fit into the boot, length and width, engine capacity and so on.
  ATs 1, 2, 3, 4, 9, 12, 13

- Boot sizes in cubic centimetres, cubic metres or cubic feet are often listed in the various car magazines which compare models. Compare the relative sizes of estates, hatchbacks and saloons. Makes can be compared to decide which one gives the largest average boot size.
  ATs 1, 8, 9, 12, 13

- National and manufacturer's data is available about fuel consumption. Compare and graph the figures available for 'urban driving', '56 miles per hour', and '75 miles per hour', these being the standards on which the data is based.
  ATs 1, 2, 3, 4, 9, 12, 13

- Compare the data for fuel consumption using the 'imperial' units of 'miles per hour' and the 'metric' units of 'litres per 100 kilometres'. Handbooks for most continental cars contain both types of data.
  ATs 1, 3, 7, 9, 12, 13,

- Useful data is easily obtainable about costs of replacement tyres and exhausts. Local advertisements list the most common models. These can be compared and the results circulated to parents!
  ATs 1, 2, 3, 4

- A repair bill from a garage is a useful source of data concerning labour costs, prices of spares and the imposition of VAT. The ability to 'read' such an invoice or bill is a useful life skill.
  ATs 1, 2, 3, 4,

- Petrol prices change continually. Survey the current costs of petrol of different grades in the local service stations.
  ATs 1, 2, 3, 4, 9, 12, 13

- Most petrol stations have a gallon/litres conversion chart attached to the pumps. Often prices are quoted in relation to either litres or gallons or both. Make a conversion chart or graph of local petrol prices.
  ATs 1, 4, 7, 8, 9, 12, 13

- Make a print of the tyre tread patterns of the staff cars. These can be compared for pattern (regular, symmetrical, naming of shapes included).
  ATs 1, 3, 9, 10

- Survey local 'pay' car parks. Examine and describe the data shown on the tickets. The machines which dispense the tickets require the use of specific combinations of coins in order to match the required fee. Examine and list the different ways in which the various parking charges could be paid if no change is given by the machine.
  ATs 1, 2, 3, 4

- Car tyres vary in size. Each size has a series of code numbers. List the different sizes and match to different makes and models of cars. Identify the meaning of a code number on a tyre such as 165 SR 13.
  ATs 1, 2, 5, 8

- Tyre pressures are measured in 'bars' or in 'pounds per square inch'. Use a car handbook to find the recommended tyre pressures in both units. Produce a line/relationship graph of the data.
  ATs 1, 2, 5, 7, 8, 9, 12, 13

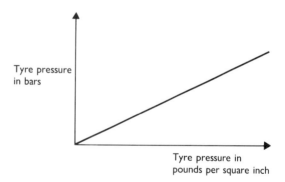

- The Highway Code lists, diagrammatically, the stopping distances in feet at various speeds in miles per hour. The data, and its subdivision into thinking distances and braking distance (which together make the total stopping distance on dry roads) can be graphed in a variety of ways. Comparison of the data with the metric equivalent is fruitful to decide which way is most amenable to memory by a driver.
  ATs 1, 8, 9, 13

A two-way chart or table

Model	Sun roof	Stereo radio	Power steering	Electric windows	Automatic gearbox
L		✓			
LX		✓			
GLX	✓	✓		✓	✓
SGLX	✓	✓	✓	✓	

■ Many parents have hired a car or van for a period of time, or the school has hired one for a trip. Local firms will supply costs and conditions for comparison of:
  (a) daily and weekly charges;
  (b) different means of transporting different numbers of people. For example, if 12 people need to travel 20 miles to an exhibition, which is the cheapest way – several cars, a minibus, or an underutilised coach?

ATs 1, 2, 3, 8

■ Cars are produced with a proliferation of models, engine sizes and levels of trim. The data can be matched with prices and shown as a two-way chart or as a series of graphs.

ATs 1, 9, 12, 13

Classroom

- Count and record the number of children who stay to school meals, go home for lunch or have a sandwich lunch in school. Record the data in a suitable way.
  ATs 1, 2, 5, 9, 12, 13

- Measure the dimensions and areas of display space available in the classroom. Is there enough for everyone to display a page of work at the same time?
  ATs 1, 8, 9, 10

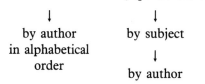

School lunch						
Home						
Sandwiches						

- Investigate ways in which the home corner or library area can be used by all children in the class without argument or overcrowding, for example a rota; maximum number, open choice; boys one day, girls next . . .
  ATs 9, 10, 11, 12, 13

- Investigate how many different types of book are kept in the classroom. Invent a means of classifying and storing the books for easy access. For example:

  Fiction and non-fiction (separate shelves)

↓	↓
by author in alphabetical order	by subject
	↓
	by author

  ATs 9, 12, 13

- Using the class groups sitting at their tables or desks, take photographs or draw pictures, then plans, of where each child sits. Discuss opposite, next to, left and right, behind, in front, facing windows, doors, blackboards and so on.
  ATs 9, 11

- Make a plan of the whole classroom without reference to scale. Discuss and record the number of groups, the numbers in each group, the items that are in fixed positions, the children who sit near to the window, the door, the blackboard and so on.
  ATs 1, 8, 9, 10, 11

- Count the number of chairs. Match one-to-one with the children. How many chairs (or children!) are spare? Investigate whether the same pattern occurs in the other classrooms.
  ATs 1, 2, 3, 5

Clothes

- Sort the children by defining the colour of a particular item of clothing. Record in a pictorial form.
  ATs 9, 12, 13

- Using real items, or if necessary pictures from magazines and mail order catalogues, sort items of clothing according to the following criteria:

  Cold weather/hot weather
  Indoor/outdoor
  School/playing out
  Rainy days/warm sunny days
  Sports and PE/or not
  Outerwear/underwear
  Record in mapping diagrams, Venn or Carroll diagrams.
  ATs 9, 12, 13

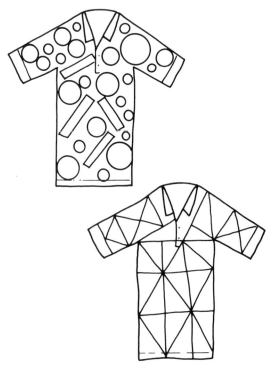

Mapping

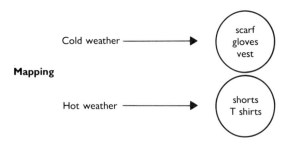

Venn

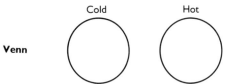

Carroll

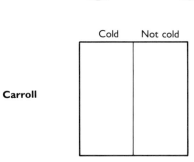

- Design some very elaborate costumes for a mathematical 'carnival'. They must be constructed and designed using mathematical shapes which are recognisable and capable of being named, for example cylinder, cuboid, cone, pyramid and so on.
  ATs 9, 10, 11

- Survey the shoe sizes of the children in the class and record in a suitable pictorial or graphical form.
  ATs 9, 12, 13

- List items of clothing which come in pairs. Do you include trousers?
  ATs 1, 2, 3, 5

- Design a sport shirt or bib for the school. Require it to show *bilateral* symmetry.
  ATs 9, 11

Communicating

- List the telephone numbers of the class members. Look for and describe any interesting patterns in the numerals used, for example 7722, 54321, and so on.
  ATs 1, 2, 4, 5

- Survey, group and graph the frequency of occurrence of certain house numbers of the members of the class.
  ATs 9, 12, 13

- Design and draw a flow chart of the sequence of actions to take if you were lost or left behind on a trip to a strange town.
  ATs 9, 11, 12, 13

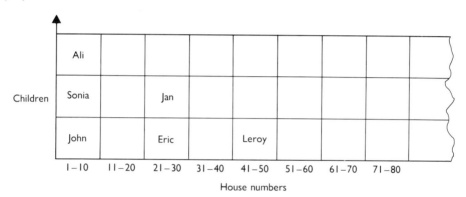

Children

		Ali						
Sonia		Jan						
John		Eric		Leroy				

1–10   11–20   21–30   31–40   41–50   51–60   61–70   71–80

House numbers

- Ask the school secretary to save all the envelopes received in the post to the school. Use the postmarks to determine the place of origin of the items. Plot these on a nationwide map. Use the scale of the map or a road atlas distance chart to find the approximate cost per kilometre of posting the letter. It would be useful to examine, for a small number of the posted items, the approximate cost of delivery of the same item by independent delivery firms.
  ATs 1, 2, 3, 4, 5, 8

- Find the current range of stamp denominations available. By combinations of one, two, three or more stamps find the possible total values of different sets. How many different ways can the cost of First Class postage of a normal letter be met by combinations of lower denomination stamps?
  ATs 1, 2, 3, 4

- Leaflets from the Post Office detail costs of letter and parcel post for packages of different weights. Weigh some items from the classroom, using either a balance or a scale and find the cost of postage of the items to places within the United Kingdom and abroad.
  ATs 1, 2, 3, 4, 8

■ Telephone charges vary according to the time of the call, its duration, and the distance of its destination. Use the data sheets provided by British Telecom to investigate the costs of calls made from the school. Is telephoning ever cheaper than writing and posting a letter, taking into account the time taken for each type of communication?

ATs 1, 2, 3, 4, 8

Decorating

■ Use a chart like the one illustrated opposite to estimate the number of rolls of wallpaper that would be needed to fully decorate the classroom.

The requirements of other rooms or corridors can be estimated in similar ways.

ATs 1, 2, 8, 9, 11, 12, 13

■ Cans of paint always show the approximate coverage of one litre. Collect some old paint cans and estimate the costs of repainting an old cupboard.

ATs 1, 3, 8

■ Find ways of cutting polystyrene tiles to fit into an awkwardly shaped space, perhaps in a walk-in cupboard.

ATs 9, 10, 11

Height of wall in metres	Perimeter of room including windows and doors (in metres)						
	9	10	11	12	13	14	15
2.0 to 2.2	4	4	5	5	5	6	6
2.2 to 2.4	4	4	5	5	6	6	6
2.4 to 2.6	4	5	5	6	6	7	7
2.6 to 2.8	5	5	6	6	7	7	8
2.8 to 3.0	5	5	6	7	7	8	8

Families

(**Note**: Because of the large number of children who have unusual family circumstances it is essential to take care in deciding what constitutes a 'normal' family structure.)

- Use family photographs, or get children to draw their families. How many family members are there? How many have different colours of hair or eyes?
  ATs 1, 2, 3, 9, 12, 13

- List the occupations of the family members. Graph the results of the survey.
  ATs 9, 12, 13

- Choose some of the occupations. Which ones require a uniform to be worn? Make an arrow diagram of uniform and non-uniform jobs in the families of the class.
  ATs 9, 12, 13

- Survey and list the names used to identify grandparents. Sort them and match with the children using mappings or arrow diagrams.
  ATs 9, 12, 13

- Make a simple time-line to show how the generations are in sequence but overlap.
  ATs 1, 2, 5, 8

- Discuss and draw a simple family tree to the grandparents' level.
  ATs 9, 12, 13

- Survey the numbers of aunts, uncles and cousins. Sort into sets of those who live locally or not.
  ATs 9, 12, 13

- Discuss and sort information about the frequency of seeing or visiting various relatives.
  ATs 9, 12, 13

- Imagine a family picnic. Discuss and decide about the amounts and sets of items needed, for example number of sandwiches, bags of crisps, drinks, cups, saucers, plates, sets of cutlery.
  ATs 1, 2, 3, 4, 9, 12, 13

- Survey the local places where the class have been for a picnic. Tally and graph the results.
  ATs 9, 12, 13

- Survey the sorts of leisure activities undertaken by the class families, for example watching football, day trips, sewing or knitting. Who takes part in different activities within each family?
  ATs 9, 12, 13

- Survey and make a chart of the favourite television programmes of a family. Discuss which programmes are watched by the whole family or individual members. Illustrate using pictures or diagrams.
  ATs 9, 12, 13

- Simulate a family sitting around a table for a meal. Use role play or a simple desk-top model to discuss such questions as who sits opposite to whom, on left or right, next door-but-one to, and so on. Examine the consequences of different seating arrangements, for example male/female, age order and so on.
  ATs 1, 5, 9, 11

Festivals

- Make a list of the religious and 'social' festivals which are part of the lives of the children in the class, bearing in mind that all classes bring to school a variety of religious and cultural backgrounds.

  Use a standard year-planner to show the dates of the festivals. This can be refined into a block graph of the twelve months of the year to show their distribution through the year in an easy-to-read form.
  ATs 1, 3, 8, 9, 12,13

- Eid-Ul-Fitr is the important Muslim festival which marks the end of Ramadan, a month of fasting. The precise date varies from year to year because it is based on the Islamic year. It takes place on the first day of the tenth month of the Islamic calendar. It can be a worthwhile exercise to relate the two calendars over the last few years.

  People send Eid 'greetings' cards to each other and they can form the basis of work in mathematical design. Being non-representational they are often symmetrical in design, or are formed by 'translation' of a shape along a line. Typical designs are shown below, but other variations are possible.
  ATs 9, 10, 11

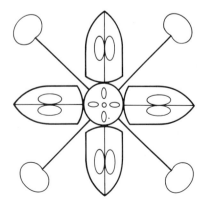

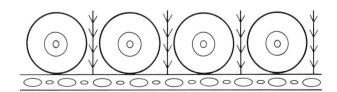

- Easter, the Christian festival, occurs on various dates depending on the lunar calendar and the date of the vernal (spring) equinox. Easter Sunday is always the first Sunday following the first full moon after the 21 March. Use a series of old diaries, which show the phases of the moon, to show how the actual dates have been calculated for given years.

  ATs 1, 2, 3, 8

- Eggs play an important symbolic role in the festival. Children can decorate hard boiled eggs in *symmetrical* designs.

  ATs 9, 10, 11

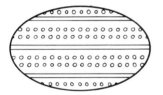

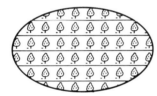

- Hold an egg rolling competition with accurate measurement of the distances achieved.

  ATs 1, 8

- Hold a class egg and spoon race using accurate measurement of times achieved.

  ATs 1,8

- Hold an Easter hat competition, basing the designs on the use of three dimensional mathematical shapes, such as the cylinder, cube, cuboid, triangular prism. Restricting the number of shapes which can be used encourages ingenuity.

  ATs 9, 10, 11

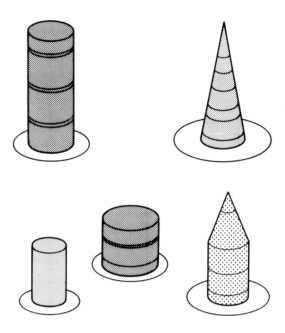

- Hot cross buns are divided into four (equal) parts, and are notionally circular in shape. Find other ways of dividing a circle into four parts of equal size.

  ATs 1, 3, 9, 10, 11

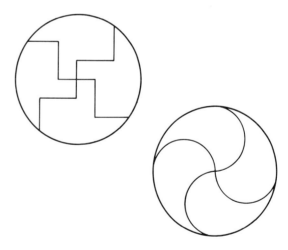

- Chinese New Year is the beginning of the lunar year in the Chinese calendar. The actual date is determined by the phases of the moon, but is usually in late January or early February. Each year of the Chinese calendar is named after an animal. They follow in a cyclical sequence, and using recent years as the example are:

First	RAT	1984
Second	OX	1985
Third	TIGER	1986
Fourth	RABBIT	1987
Fifth	DRAGON	1988
Sixth	SNAKE	1989
Seventh	HORSE	1990
Eighth	RAM	1991
Ninth	MONKEY	1992
Tenth	COCKEREL	1993
Eleventh	DOG	1994
Twelfth	PIG	1995

Children can trace their own, or their families', year-animal to see if there is any pattern.

ATs 1, 2, 3, 5

- Make a Chinese dragon head using a limited number of plane and solid shapes, for example cuboid, circle, triangle.

  ATs 9, 10, 11

- Make Chinese lanterns, using the techniques of folding and cutting. Restrict the number of measurement or 'mathematical' techniques which can be used. Encourage children to 'name' the mathematical structures they have made and used.

  ATs 9, 10, 11

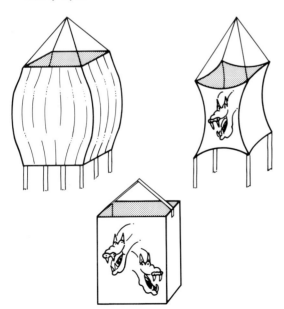

- Make a two-dimensional symmetrical Christmas tree for the classroom wall. The basic outline actually looks symmetrical. This can be enhanced by the use of balancing colours, shapes and sizes of 'decorations' made for the tree. A discussion and analysis of the differences between the real tree and the class model will make full use of the vocabulary of shape and number. Survey opinions about real and artificial trees among staff and children and illustrate graphically.

  ATs 9, 10, 11

- Using a box of any size, get the children to investigate the size of a piece of paper which will 'wrap' the box. Set the requirement that the minimum area of paper should be used, that the sheet should be 'whole' but of any shape. Hold a class competition using 1 cm or 2 cm squared paper to allow easier checking of the area of the wrapping.

  ATs 1, 8, 9, 10, 11

- Chanukah is the Jewish festival of lights. It is an eight-day festival and most Jewish homes have a menorah, which is an eight-candle, symmetrical candelabrum. Children can be asked to construct such a shape as a drawing at first, using a pair of compasses and ruler, and then to attempt to make a model of the item.

During Chanukah many Jewish children are given a specially designed spinning top called a dreidel. The finished shape looks like this:

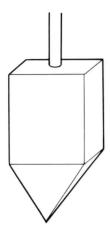

Its 'net' can be of this shape but it could be constructed using interlocking plane shapes such as 'polydrons' or separate rectangles and equilateral triangles joined using transparent sticky tape.

ATs 9, 10, 11

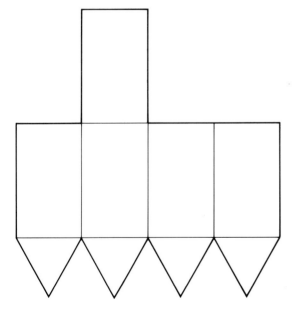

■ Halloween always occurs on 31 October of each year. Traditionally it is a time for model making and mask making. Encourage children to design and make witches' hats so that the construction of a 'cone' can be investigated. Make symmetrical masks which use mathematical shapes for the cut-outs and stick-ons.

ATs 9, 10, 11

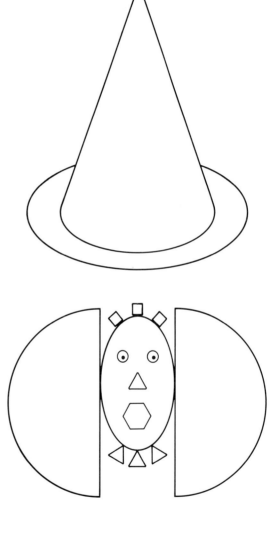

45

Flying

Collect pictures of things which fly. Sort them into categories such as jet aeroplanes, other aircraft (for example helicopters or propeller driven aircraft), birds, kites, parachutes, insects and so on.

Most can be placed under a single category and recorded as a simple Venn diagram or other representation. Decisions would have to be made about 'flying fish' or 'flying squirrels', or balloons, and it is possible that some can be classified under more than one heading which would require the use of overlapping sets on the Venn Diagram.

ATs 9, 12, 13

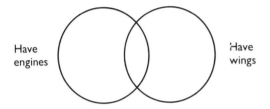

	Have engines	Do not have engines
Have wings	aeroplane	bird
Do not have wings	helicopter	parachute

Use a variety of airborne seeds, such as sycamore. Hold a competition outside on a windy day to determine, and measure, the distance travelled and therefore the 'champion' seed! Record the data in tabular form and as a graph.

ATs 1, 8, 9, 12, 13

The structure of a flying seed can be reproduced by making a paper spinner and testing and recording its 'flight' in a similar way. Use a small rectangle of stiff paper and a paper clip or lump of Blu-tack as ballast.

ATs 9, 10, 11

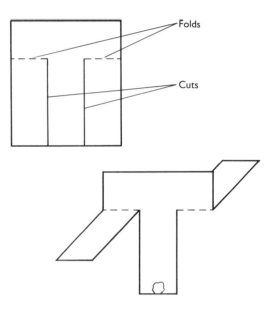

Make paper darts of a variety of designs. Test and record their flight in a suitable way for the age of the children.

ATs 1, 8, 9, 10, 11

Hold a competition, with accurate or approximate measurements, of distances the group can throw a variety of objects of different mass, shape and flight characteristics. These can be such things as a polystyrene cube, a Frisbee, a counter, a feather and so on. Record the results in tabular or graphical form.

ATs 1, 8, 9, 12, 13

Food

- Make a list of things the group likes to eat, or hates to eat. Sort them into two sets using the class or group information.
  ATs 9, 12, 13

Food	Eyes	Tongue	Hands	Nose	Ears
Crisps	✓	✓			✓
Smarties					

- Investigate sweets. List and discuss the senses used to decide whether we like them, for example eyes to look at the packet, tongue to taste the flavour, hands to touch and examine the texture, nose to smell, and ears to listen to the rattle or crunch. Match the senses to some everyday foods and illustrate as a chart.
  ATs 9, 12, 13

- Run a class competition to attempt to identify food items by smell alone. Because texture is an important factor in the recognition of foods it is worthwhile liquidising any obvious examples. For example a basic list of possibilities could consist of:

  Drinks: tea, coffee, chocolate, cocoa, Horlicks, fruit juices, vinegar and so on.

  Fruits: banana, apple, orange, pear, and so on.

  Vegetables: carrot, onion, lettuce, potato and so on.

  The lists can be sorted into sets and recorded using Venn or Carroll diagrams, or in a graph showing the number of children able to identify each food.
  ATs 9, 12, 13

- Make lists of everyday foods dividing them into two categories, i.e. sweet/not sweet, fruit/not fruit, meat/vegetables, hard/soft, available in cans or not, available frozen or not and so on. The results can be recorded in an attribute chart, or other visual mode to encourage ease of analysis by the child.
  ATs 9, 12, 13

Food	Sweet	Not sweet	Fruit	Not fruit	Meat	Not meat	Hard	Soft	Canned	Not canned	Frozen	Not frozen
Pineapples	✓		✓			✓		✓	✓	✓		
Carrots												

- Discuss and list the vegetables normally eaten by the families of the children in the class. Given the renewed interest in healthy eating this is likely to be a more extensive list than at first expected. Confirmation of the names and countries of origin of the more exotic vegetables can be found in leaflets issued by the major supermarket chains. Sort the vegetables listed into various categories and record in a suitable pictorial form. Such categories might be:

Countries of origin.

Which bit do we eat – leaves, roots, underground stalk (potato) or flowers?

Predominant colour?

Eaten raw or cooked?

ATs 9, 12, 13

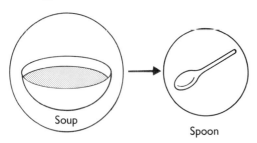

Soup   Spoon

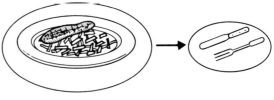

Fish and Chips   Knife and Fork

- Make a plan of where the members of each family sit when they have a meal together. Discuss and draw a table setting for a family to eat together. What cutlery is needed and used for different courses? Illustrate diagrammatically using mappings or arrow diagrams. Discuss and sort items and their places, for example fork on the left.

ATs 1, 2, 9, 12, 13

- Systematic counting of the numbers of pips in oranges over a period of time can be used to show a 'curve of distribution' and illustrates which is the 'most likely' number of pips in an orange – an illustration of the idea of average or a middling value.

ATs 1, 2, 5, 9, 12, 13, 14

The results would look something like this:

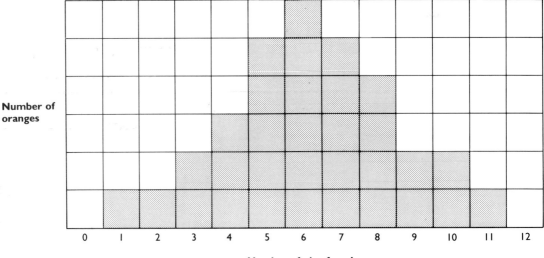

Number of oranges

0   1   2   3   4   5   6   7   8   9   10   11   12

Number of pips found

48

- Using packets of sweets which contain different shapes, such as Licorice Allsorts, sort the sweets into shapes to be matched with large wood or plastic solids of a cylinder, a cube, a cuboid, a triangular prism and so on. If possible use the correct terminology throughout. The relative quantities of each shape can be counted and recorded in pictorial form. Added motivation of children can be gained by allowing the consumption of the sweet if the child can give it its correct mathematical name.

  ATs 9, 10, 12, 13

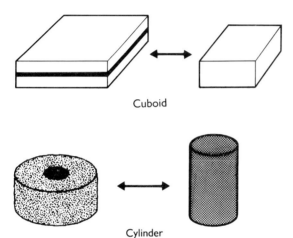

Cuboid

Cylinder

- Collect a range of spoons, scoops and ladles. All are used for a variety of purposes to convey and/or measure dry and liquid quantities. Sort and label them according to function. Spoons of different dry goods, such as rice or sand can be compared for relative mass. Spoons can be ranked in order of size (capacity or length). They can also be sorted and recorded according to material used, for example plastic, metal, wood.

  ATs 1, 8, 9, 12, 13

- Borrow a real menu from a local take-away or cafe. Discuss children's favourite meals and find total prices.

  ATs 1, 2, 3, 4

- Survey the costs of different soft drinks from auto-dispenser machines, supermarkets, and small local shops, as well as the fast food chains. The various cans, bottles or cartons can be brought into the classroom and displayed with prices from the different sources. The data can be analysed in a variety of ways, for example ordering according to price, capacity, value for money, and recorded using diagrams and graphs.

  ATs 9, 12, 13

Homes

■ Using the children's own homes or a local road/estate survey the numbers of different sorts of homes, for example detached houses, detached bungalows, semi-detached houses, semi-detached bungalows, terraced homes, flats, maisonettes. Graph the results of the survey i.e. numbers of different types, arrow diagrams matching type to the children in the class.
ATs 9, 12, 13

■ Photograph or draw pairs of semi-detached homes. Examine and discuss the *symmetry* (or near symmetry) of the designs.
ATs 9, 10, 11

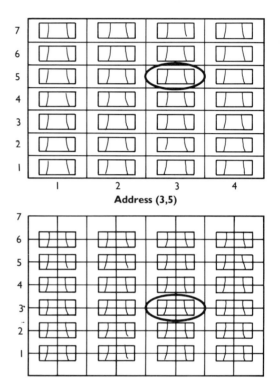

Address (3,5)

Co-ordinates (5,3)

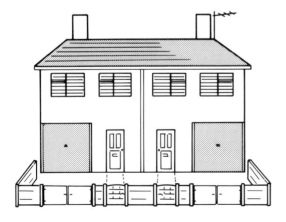

■ Find a way of counting the number of steps/stairs in a block of flats by counting just one flight and multiplying by the number of floors. In a similar way the number of windows can be counted as an array on units arranged in a rectangular pattern. Work on addresses and coordinates can be done to identify positions.
ATs 1, 2, 7

■ Survey the number of windows in a series of homes. Relate this data to the type of home, for example detached bungalow.
ATs 1, 2, 3, 4, 5, 9, 12, 13

- Collect a series of pictures of doors from a DIY superstore. Sort the designs into types, for example panelled, glazed and so on. Discuss and draw the different designs. Survey a local street to try to match the designs to the actual doors used. Design a door.
  ATs 9, 10, 11

- Survey the kinds of roofs of the children's homes. Sort them into types such as tiles, slates, felt, thatch. These can be further sub-divided into colours and whether flat or pitched. The information can be recorded using Venn or Carroll diagrams, leading up to three overlapping characteristics.
  ATs 9, 10, 12, 13

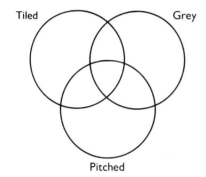

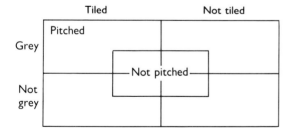

- Survey the availability of gardens in the class sample or a nearby street. These can be sub-divided into categories such as front, back, side, large, small, shared/communal.
  ATs 9, 12, 13

- Survey the materials used for the construction of the walls of the homes. The data can be sub-divided into such categories as brick, stone, concrete and wood. This data can be related to some extent to the age of the property. Sketch or make a scale drawing on the floor plans of the homes lived in by the children. Label each room. The location of items such as the windows, cooker and bath can be noted using symbols and a key.
  ATs 1, 8, 9, 12, 13

- Discuss and examine reasons why architects use the symbols like the ones below for doors. (To show the direction of opening and the amount of space taken up by the opening door(s).) Examine other symbols used in plans.
  ATs 1, 5, 8

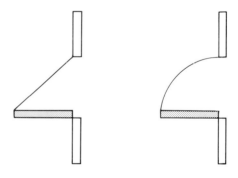

- Draw and label a plan (either a sketch or a scale drawing) of a child's bedroom. Each item should be shown either as symbols or actual representations. Possible re-arrangements can be examined to fulfil given criteria, for example open space for a model railway, radiator not obstructed, power points not covered.
  ATs 1, 8, 9, 10, 11

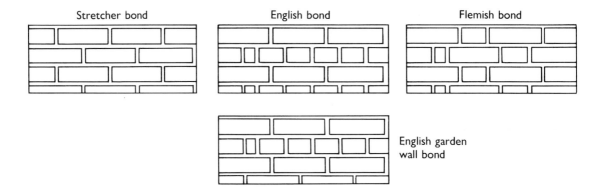

Stretcher bond   English bond   Flemish bond

English garden
wall bond

■ Examine a series of brick bonding patterns such as the ones above.

Use Lego or Centicubes to create some of the patterns. They can be copied on to squared paper or, rubbings can be made of the patterns.
ATs 9, 10, 11

■ List the different occupations of the people who contribute to the building of a home, for example plasterer, bricklayer, painter and so on. Make a survey, perhaps using a DIY guidebook to match and record the different tools used by the various people.
ATs 9, 12, 13

■ Contact one or more of the DIY kitchen suppliers. They produce scaled grid paper and cut-out shapes for their units. Using the child's home kitchen, or a small room in school, design a kitchen to fit the space. (Most children are very surprised by the cost!)
ATs 1, 8, 9, 10, 11

■ Borrow a doll's house. They have a very simple room layout. Given a limited supply of miniature furniture the house can be planned and furnished in a variety of ways. Opinions of the children can be collected concerning the 'best' design and a systematic ranking made and discussed.
ATs 9, 10, 11

■ Use a large scale map of the area. Plot the homes of each child. Record the addresses and post codes. Draw and measure routes from home to friends' houses or to school.
ATs 1, 8, 9, 11

■ If you are lucky one child may have a spiral staircase at home. In fact it is a helix, since a spiral is flat, but can stimulate discussion and drawing of both.
ATs 9, 10, 11

■ Use estate agent's advertisements in local papers. Compare prices of different sorts of houses in different locations. Plot them on a large scale map.
ATs 1, 2, 3, 4, 8

Kitchen

- Use a selection of real kitchen utensils, Sort them according to function, for example cooking, straining, measuring, pouring and so on. Record pictorially using arrow diagrams.
  ATs 9, 12, 13

- Utensils can also be sorted according to the material used in their construction, including those with more than one material used, for example a knife with a plastic or wooden handle.
  ATs 9, 12, 13

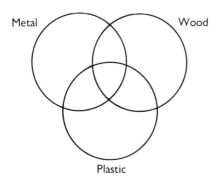

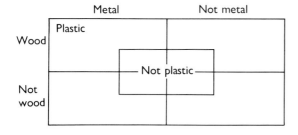

- Set out a random, but limited number of knives, forks and spoons of various sizes. Ask children to arrange some of the items in a way which is suitable for the eating of a given meal.

  Investigate the ways in which other place settings can be made – by translation along the edge of a table, and rotation to go round a corner. What happens if you try to reflect a place setting on to the opposite side of the table?
  ATs 9, 10, 11, 12, 13

- Rank a set of spoons of different sizes according to capacity using the smallest as the 'standard' but arbitrary unit for checking the others.
  ATs 1,8

- Use a paper napkin or serviette. Find ways to fold it which will produce squares, rectangles or triangles of different sizes. (See R. Harbin's book '*Origami*', Hodder & Stoughton.)
  ATs 9, 10, 11

- Order the capacities of various household cups, glasses or plastic beakers.
  ATs 1, 8

- Although the most important kitchen item for weighing is a balance, encourage children to weigh items on a spring balance or on a pressure scale which shows the 'weight' on a dial or scale.
  ATs 1,8

- Compare the mass or 'weight' of identical pots filled with different dry products such as sugar, peas, rice or cornflakes.
  ATs 1,8

- Allowing a limited range of items such as one drink, one round of sandwiches, one biscuit from a packet available commercially, and one item of fruit, find the total amount in bottles, loaves, packets and so on to make snacks of equal quantity for the group or class. This can be costed accurately and prices compared in different shops. It is advisable to actually create and eat the picnic to lend reality to the exercise.
  ATs 1, 2, 3, 4

- List all the items which turn or rotate during use in the kitchen, for example a mincer, or mixer or whisk. Sort a range of items according to the type of motion they use, or are used with.
  ATs 9, 10, 11

- Investigate patterns used in kitchen design – doors, floor tiles or vinyl covering, wallpaper, wall tiles, blinds, radiators and so on.
  ATs 9, 10, 11

- There are many simple recipes suitable for safe preparation and cooking by children of all ages. Although there is no intention to produce a cookery book in these pages, it is worth pointing out that many recipes can be simplified and adapted to use 'cups', 'spoonsful', or similar to reduce the problems of accurate weighing. The simplest way is to adapt a recipe to read something like: 'Take two eggs. Then take enough flour to balance two eggs . . . '. Depending on the age of the children recipes using both ounces and grams (but not at the same time!) can be used.
  ATs 1, 4, 8

Music

■ Sort and record, in pictorial or graphical form, 'real' and home-made musical instruments into the following groups:
Shakers: rattles, tambourines etc.
Pluckers: guitars, banjos, etc.
Scrapers: violins etc.
Bangers: drums etc.
Blowers: recorders, whistles etc.
Chimers: bells, xylophones, glockenspiels etc.
ATs 9, 12, 13

■ Fill a variety of containers made of plastic, glass, pottery and wood with water. Fill them to the same level. Compare and record on a chart the type of sound they make when struck, for example loud, soft, sharp, dull, high, low, 'sweet', 'grating', 'unpleasant'.
ATs 1, 8, 9, 12

■ Fill a variety of identical glass containers to different levels. Place them in order of pitch. Record by drawing or by words or symbols. Get the children to attempt to match them to the nearest note on a piano or recorder.
ATs 1, 8, 9, 12

■ Examine the 'pop charts' published in many newspapers. Survey changing positions in the rankings over a period of one month.
ATs 1, 2, 3, 4

■ Pick one 'single and chart its progress over time, for example:
Week 1 – Start at number 40
Week 2 – Up 13 to 27
Week 3 – Down 2 to 29
Week 4 – Up 19 to 10 etc.
This can be graphed as a continuous line.
ATs 1, 7, 9, 12, 13

■ Survey the duration of the playing time of current 'singles'. Which one provides best 'value for money'? Design a programme of consecutive songs and instrumentals to last for a specific duration.
ATs 1, 3, 5, 8

■ List the 'length' or duration of various notes, for example:
semiquaver – ¼ beat
quaver – ½ beat
crotchet – 1 beat
minim – 2 beats
semibreve – 4 beats

If the children are capable, the dotted notes can be featured as well.

Using suitable pieces of music decide on and list the number of 'beats' in various phrases.
ATs 1, 2, 5

■ Play two pieces of music, one with a fast rhythm and one with a slow rhythm. Discuss and decide which has the greater duration and how it can be estimated. It is worth noting here that saying 'one-elephant', 'two-elephants' and so on gives a good estimate of the passage of seconds.
ATs 1, 8

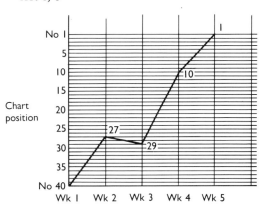

- Ask everyone to close their eyes and keep them closed for one minute. Record the numbers of children who open their eyes before 30 seconds, 45 seconds, 60 seconds have passed. Graph the results in a suitable way.
  ATs 1,8

- Record the members of the class or group saying aloud the same sentence. Make a graph of the differences in pitch from highest to lowest, perhaps using 3 or 4 groupings to allow for those which are indistinguishable. The activity can bc carried on at home to record and analyse families and friends.
  ATs 9, 12, 13

- Number the consecutive 'white' keys on a piano or keyboard from 1 to 9. Using the children's telephone numbers, dates of birth and so on, construct melodies by playing the 'numbers'. Play guessing games to find the number by hearing the melody.
  ATs 1, 2, 5

- List all the 'musical' words which the children know, sorting them under letters of the alphabet.
  ATs 9, 12, 13

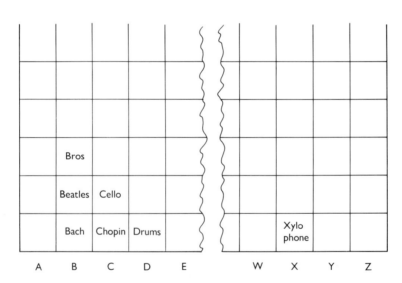

56

Newspapers

- Survey, tally and record the newspapers taken by the staff and children's families of the school.
  ATs 9, 12, 13

- All newspapers have an issue number. Find the approximate date of the first issue by counting back.
  ATs 1, 2, 3, 4

- Divide the content of a newspaper into categories, such as Sport, Advertisements, Home News, Foreign News, Photographs and so on. Find a way of measuring the amount of space devoted to each category and record in an appropriate way.
  ATs 1, 8, 12, 13

- Survey the length of the words used on the front page of several newspapers. Tally, tabulate, and graph the data in an appropriate way.
  ATs 1, 2, 3, 4, 9, 12, 13

- Weigh several different newspapers of the same date. Discuss which gives greatest 'value for money' in grams per penny.
  ATs 1, 2, 3, 4, 8

- Find the total print area of several newspapers of the same date. Discuss which gives greatest 'value for money' in square centimetres per penny.
  ATs 1, 2, 3, 4, 8

Ourselves

- Make a list of the children in the class. How many children are there? How many eyes, hands, feet?
  ATs 1, 2, 3, 4, 5

- Sort the children by eye colour using a limited range, blue, brown, green, hazel, grey. They can be drawn, coloured and mounted as a chart, block graph or pictograph.
  ATs 9, 12, 13

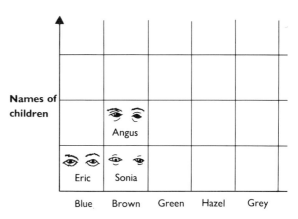

Names of children

Blue Brown Green Hazel Grey

Eye colours

- Sort the children by hair colour using a limited range of possibilities, for example black, brown, fair, ginger. Record in a suitable pictorial or graphical form.
  ATs 9, 12, 13

- Draw self-portraits using the correct 'colours' for eyes and hair. These can then be sorted in a variety of ways.
  ATs 9, 10, 11

- Outline the body shapes of the children on large sheets of paper. Sort them according to height, width, those wearing trousers, those wearing shorts, width of the head or waist and so on.
  ATs 1, 8, 9, 12, 13

- Find the area of each child's body outline. This can be done in a variety of ways, for example chalking the outline on a brick wall and counting 'bricks' as units of area, or getting the children to lie down on newspaper and using a direct comparison method relating one group member's area to another. Greater accuracy can be achieved (but is it worthwhile?) by standing the child against squared paper and counting small squares. It is important to note that we measure in 'square' units as a matter of convenience and standardisation. Other tessellating shapes are equally suitable.
  ATs 1, 8, 9, 10, 11

- Trace around hands on squared paper. Cut out the outlines and compare areas first by overlaying and then by counting squares. A similar activity can be done using triangular grid or rectangular grid paper to illustrate different ways of measuring amounts of space occupied by a shape.
  ATs 1, 8, 9, 10, 11

- Outline and cut out shapes of feet. Use the shapes for observation of patterns, for example *symmetry* of left and right, *translation* of left foot followed by left foot. Patterns and sequences of left-right-left-right-can be described in words, pictures or symbols.
  ATs 9, 10, 11

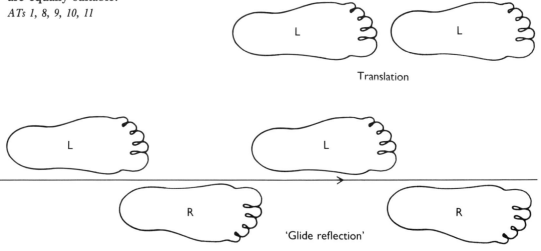

Symmetry

Translation

'Glide reflection'

58

- Draw around the outline of the child's shoe. Overlay the foot outline of the child to show how one fits inside the other.
- Discuss whether shoes 'fit' and what is meant by a 'good' fit.

  ATs 9, 10, 11

- Measure and record the children's feet. The dimensions and shoe sizes can be recorded for sorting and analysis using Venn diagrams. Data can be recorded in this way before sorting and pictorial representation.

  ATs 9, 12, 13

- Compare the mass/weight of children using 'to the nearest whole kilogram' as the unit of measurement. Graph in an appropriate way.

  ATs 1, 8, 9, 12, 13

- Use previous school registers or admissions books of the school. Find the three most popular names for boys and girls in each previous year available. Discuss whether the names have changed over the period (which they almost certainly will have done). The most popular names can be recorded in a variety of ways. Use a simple time-line to place the generations of a family and record with the popular names of the period. Grandparents and other older people in the community could be asked to remember and note the names of friends and families to confirm (or not) the results of the register survey.

  ATs 1, 2, 3, 4, 8, 9, 12, 13

Name	Length		Width		Girth		Area		Size
	L	R	L	R	L	R	L	R	

Packages

- Using standard packages, for example a Cornflakes or Weetabix box, open them out to make the net. Use thin card to make similar packages in which all the dimensions are halved or doubled. Measure and record what happens to the surface area of the packages. Measure and record the consequences for the volume/capacity of each container.
  ATs 1, 8, 9, 10, 11

- Discuss and list the food, drink, and utensil requirements for a picnic for four people. Collect or make true-size packages and containers of the required items. Choose or make a box into which all the items will fit without leaving any empty space. Discuss what should be done about round items, for example a cake.
  ATs 9, 10, 11

- The ingredients for a cake occupy a much smaller volume before cooking than they do after cooking. Ask the children to investigate ways in which the increase in 'space occupied' can be measured. (The solution is based on the fact that the base of the tin remains constant. Its area can be measured by counting squares on a tracing on squared paper. The pre-cooked height and the cooked height can be measured to compare the two volumes).
  ATs 1, 4, 8

- Use Centicubes to find the approximate capacity of some small boxes, such as match boxes or sweet/chocolate containers. The volume of a single match or a single sweet/chocolate can then be approximated by dividing by the number each container holds. Use of a calculator and some awareness of sensible answers (i.e. with a reasonable level of accuracy) is required.
  ATs 1, 8, 9, 10

- Shoe boxes are commonly available in large quantities if requested. Investigate the range of shoe boxes acquired. Are they all the same size despite differences in shoe sizes? If so, why? Using thin card, the child can make a shoe box of identical size (but without a lid) and examine its capacity, after estimating.
  ATs 1, 8, 9, 10, 11

- Investigate the wrapping of different shaped 'presents'. Try to find the minimum amount of paper needed to completely wrap a given solid.
  ATs 1, 8, 9, 10, 11

- Compare the value for money of different brands of common items such as flour, baked beans, lemonade, washing-up liquid, beefburgers and margarine. Compare the amounts you get for one penny, which is the weight divided by the cost, or the costs for one gram of each of the products.
  ATs 1, 2, 3, 4, 8

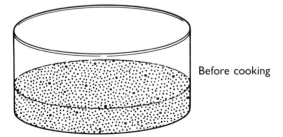

Before cooking

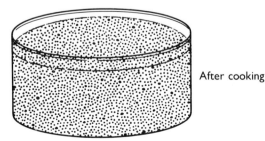

After cooking

■ Investigate hexominoes to decide which of them can be folded to make a closed box. If the patterns of 'dice' dots are marked on the hexominoes (which are of course the nets of possible cubes) the exercise becomes even more interesting and fruitful.

■ Use some actual packets or tins which show the net weight, i.e. the weight of the contents. Remove the packaging and find the actual weight of the contents as accurately as possible. Check the validity of the net weight as specified on the wrapping. Note that it is almost always a little more than the stated weight.

ATs 1, 2, 3, 4, 8

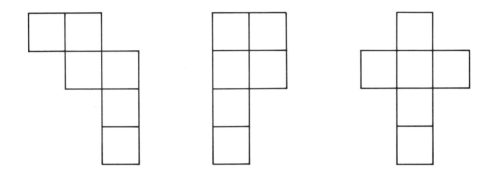

How many other hexominoes are there?

ATs 9, 10, 11

Paper

■ There is an international agreement which has fixed the sizes of paper available to people in shops and from wholesalers. This does not include the publishers who invent their own dimensions for a book so that it is different to others and will be distinctive on a shelf!

The relationships between the agreed sizes are shown opposite. Use these relationships to investigate, and create, sheets of standard sizes using pieces of (the most commonly available) A4 sheets. These can be used to illustrate fractions since A1 has half the area of A0, A2 has half the area of A1, and so on.

ATs 1, 2, 3, 4, 8, 9, 10, 11

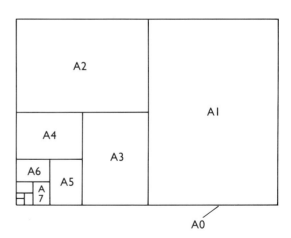

- Investigate envelope sizes in a similar way, finding envelopes into which a standard sheet of, say, A4 or A5 will fit unfolded, folded once, folded twice, and other possibilities.
  ATs 1, 2, 8, 9, 10, 11

- Open out a standard envelope to investigate its overall dimensions and positions of the flaps. Encourage the children to design and make an envelope into which a piece of paper of given dimension will fit.
  ATs 1, 8, 9, 10, 11

Park and Countryside

- A random selection of leaves and fruits can be collected. These can then be sorted and matched using reference books for identification. The results can be recorded on Venn diagrams, Carroll diagrams or a simple branching 'tree' diagram.
  ATs 1, 3, 4, 9, 12, 13

- Using a selection of leaves, make drawings and tracings to highlight symmetry and, using squared paper with squares of various sizes, comparisons of area.
  ATs 1, 8, 9, 10, 11

- There are always some trees in every neighbourhood. The approximate age of a large tree can be found by measuring the circumference of the tree at a height of about 150 cm. Multiplying the circumference by 2 and then dividing by 5 gives an approximate age in years.
  ATs 1, 3, 8

- Investigate/discuss ways in which the approximate number of leaves on a tree can be estimated.
  ATs 1, 4

- Investigate the numbers of people who work in the park, including hours of work and range of jobs done.
  ATs 1, 3, 4

- Using conkers or acorns, find the mass of ten, then use a calculator to find an approximate (average?) mass of one. In a similar way the average diameter and circumference can be found, the former measured using callipers or the blocks and ruler method, and the latter using string.
  ATs 1, 3, 4, 8

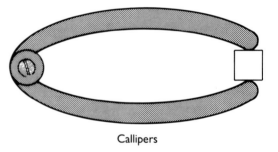

Callipers

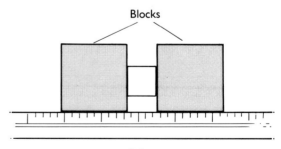

Blocks

Ruler

- If the season is suitable, examine the patterns of the formal gardens/flower beds so common in municipal parks. Look for patterns of repetition, rotation, translation and multilateral symmetry. Colour, as well as shape, is often used in the structure of the garden. Copy the designs using squared paper or pegboards with pegs of different colours.
  ATs 9, 10, 11

- Most parks have large and small fences surrounding various features. These can be examined for patterns of tessellation and translation. The designs can be copied on to grid paper of various designs.
  ATs 9, 10, 11

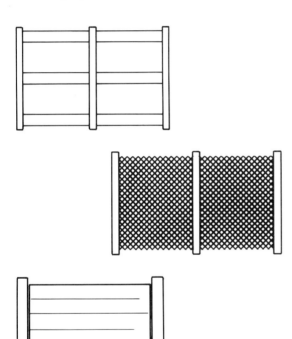

- Choose a particular seasonal growing flower which is widely available. Measure and/or compare the lengths of leaves, petals, stems. Count the number of flowers growing in a particular patch, field or small area.
  ATs 1, 3, 4, 8

- Visit the children's play area of a park. Examine and sketch the structure of the equipment, for example use of triangles for rigidity, the type and range of 'swing' or up/down movement of the items. Some can be constructed in the classroom using straws and pipe-cleaners or rolls of newspaper.
  ATs 9, 10, 11

- Make a plan of all or part of the park, using 'strides' as the unit measurement. This can be compared with a large scale plan of the area. If the park is suitable, an interesting walk can be designed and measured, with directions clearly designated. A commentary can be tape-recorded.
  ATs 1, 3, 4, 8

- Survey a sample of people who might use the park. Sub-divide the data in a variety of ways, for example visit the park daily, only at weekends, only in summer and so on. The same survey could be used to find numbers who use the park for different purposes, for example jogging, football, bowls, walking. The data can be recorded in tables and illustrated graphically.
  ATs 9, 12, 13

- Many parks make charges for different activities such as boating, tennis, bowls and mini-golf. Investigate and work out an activity day using the facilities of the park. What is the total cost and relative 'value for money'? Compare graphically the children's concepts of what would constitute an interesting day in the park and what it would cost.

  Within the classroom, survey the location of, and journeys to, municipal parks, country parks/stately homes, safari parks.
  ATs 1, 2, 3, 4, 8, 9, 11

Pets

- Survey the numbers of pets kept by each family. Graph the results in an arrow diagram, picture graph or block graph.
  ATs 9, 12, 13

- Survey the kinds of pets kept by each family. Graph the results.
  ATs 9, 12, 13

- Survey the names given to pets. Match the names to different sorts of pets.
  ATs 9, 12, 13

- Survey the ages of the pets kept by the children. Usually parents have a very good knowledge of the amount of time a particular pet has been in the house!
  ATs 1, 8, 9, 12, 13

- Taking one pet at a time, list the kinds of foods required. Draw an arrow diagram to display the different types of food.
  ATs 9, 12, 13

- Taking one pet at a time, record the mass/weight of food consumed in a day or week. Compare the results for different pets. The same can be done for the amount of water consumed in a day or week.
  ATs 1, 2, 3, 4, 8

- Find out and compare the different costs of taking a pet to a veterinary surgery. There is always a selection in or near to a town.
  ATs 1, 2, 3, 4, 8

- Make a flow diagram of the best route to take from the school to the nearest (or cheapest?) veterinary surgery.
  ATs 9, 12, 13

- List the basic needs of a pet, for example food, water, shelter, cleaning/maintenance, exercise. Make a chart of the relative importance of the different needs for different pets.
  ATs 9, 12, 13

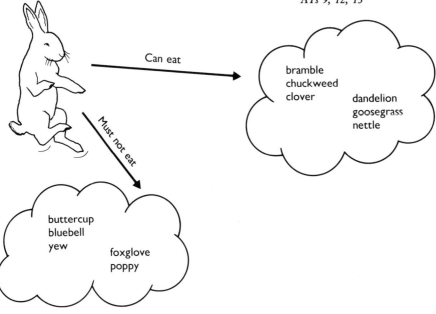

Can eat

bramble
chuckweed
clover
dandelion
goosegrass
nettle

Must not eat

buttercup
bluebell
yew
foxglove
poppy

- Make drawings or use magazine/catalogue pictures of a variety of hutches, kennels, cages and baskets. Match, record and display in relation to the different pets.
  ATs 9, 12, 13

- Using reference books, find and record the life span of various pets. Rank them in order and record on a chart. Measure and record the length and mass of a variety of pets kept by the class. Discuss the relative sizes. Are short pets always the lightest? Draw a scattergraph to check the relationship.
  ATs 1, 8, 9, 12, 13

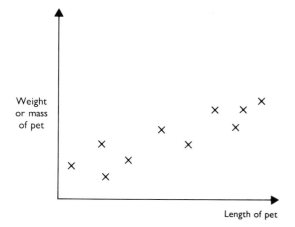

- Make a combined chart of the major facts about each pet under the headings of food, shelter, maintenance needs, size, cost to purchase, costs to keep. On the basis of the relative information decide upon relative ease to feed, shelter, exercise etc., depending on the local situation with regard to local conditions (for example type of housing, amount of open space nearby).
  ATs 9, 12, 13

- Visit the local vet. Survey the relative numbers of different sorts of pets seen by a vet in a typical day.
  ATs 9, 12, 13

- Contact the PDSA, the RSPCA or the Guide Dogs For The Blind Association. They have information packs and statistics of the numbers of animals dealt with which can be discussed and analysed mathematically.
  ATs 1, 2, 3, 8

Pooh sticks

- Play Pooh Sticks using a set of identical objects but in different situations:

Distance covered in	Canal	River	Pond
10 secs			
20 secs			
30 secs			
40 secs			
50 secs			
60 secs			

Record in tabular form and in a graphical form suitable for the age of the child.
ATs 1, 8, 9, 12, 13

- Play Pooh Sticks using a variety of different materials in a single situation:

Distance covered in	Wood block	Straw	Plastic bag
10 secs			
20 secs			
30 secs			
40 secs			
50 secs			
60 secs			

Record in tabular form and as graphs suitable for the age of the child.
ATs 1, 8, 9, 12, 13

Postcodes

- A postcode has a specific structure which is consistent throughout the whole country. Thomson's Local Directories list all the streets, and their postcodes for any town in the country. For example:

Investigate the postcodes of the children in the class, their friends and relations, and of incoming mail to the school office.
ATs 1, 2, 4, 5

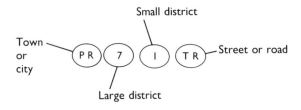

Pyramids and Egyptians

- Use interlocking plane shapes, such as Polydrons, to build solids of pyramids.
  ATs 9, 10

- Use pre-cut cardboard triangles and squares to build pyramids by joining with sticky tape.
  ATs 9, 10

Regular tetrahedron
(triangular-based pyramid)

Square-based pyramid (Egyptian)

ATS 9,10

- Use pre-drawn nets of pyramids, with flaps, to construct pyramids.
  ATs 9, 10

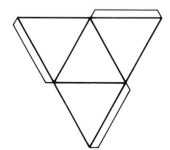

- Use pre-drawn nets of pyramids, without flaps. The children should decide the location of the flaps, draw and cut out the net and construct the solid of a pyramid.
  ATs 9, 10

- Use reference books to find the height of a specimen pyramid. Compare this height to that of a child, the school, the nearest tall building etc.
  ATs 1, 8, 9, 13

- The pyramids are not smooth faced, but are constructed from blocks of stone piled in the correct relation to each other. Construct a pyramid using small blocks of equal dimensions.
  ATs 1, 5, 9, 10

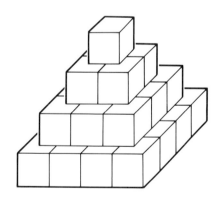

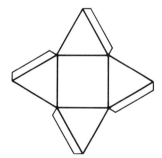

- Build a 'skeleton' of a pyramid using straws and pipe-cleaners to join the edges. Alternatively, tightly rolled newspaper of a constant size makes 'sticks'. These can be joined using Sellotape.

  ATs 9, 10, 11

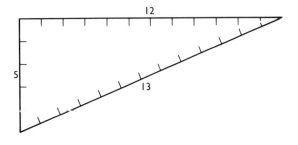

- The Egyptian rope stretchers used a rope 12 units in length, knotted at intervals of 3, 4, and 5 units, which, when stretched by holding the knots, produced a right angle which could be used to check verticals, and the 'squareness' of a base. Make such a rope and use it to check the angles of structures in the classroom.

  An extension of this is to find some other subdivisions of a rope which will also produce a right angle when stretched. For information, the main ones are: (3, 4, 5); (5, 12, 13); (7, 24, 25) (8, 15, 17); (9, 40, 41); (12, 35, 37); and (20, 21, 29).

  ATs 1, 2, 3, 5, 8, 9, 10

Routes and trips

- The use of compass directions can be reinforced by examining local maps with places marked which are known to the children. Their relative locations can be analysed and recorded using four, eight or sixteen points of the compass, depending upon ability.

  ATs 9,11

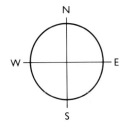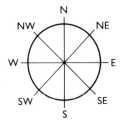

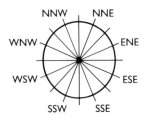

- Survey the means of transport used by children to get to school. Sort into categories and draw a suitable graph.

  ATs 9, 12, 13

MODE	TALLY	TOTAL
Walk	ⅢⅢ ⅢⅢ ⅢⅢ	15
Car	ⅠⅠⅠ	3
Aeroplane		0
Submarine		0
Elephant		0
Skateboard	ⅢⅢ ⅢⅢ ⅢⅢ ⅢⅢ	20

- Using children who live in a particular road, investigate the comparative amount of time taken to get to school using different modes of transport, for example on foot, on a bicycle, on a bus, or by car. The results do not always back up the expectations of the children. An interesting

long-term comparison can be made between time taken under different weather conditions, in different seasons, or from another road equidistant from the school.
ATs 9, 12, 13

■ Use local bus timetables to examine routes and times to local places of interest such as shops, the library, the cinema and the sports centre. Such routes can be compared in terms of distance and time in using a car, or going on foot, or, for greater distances, by train.
ATs 1, 8, 9, 12, 13

■ Ask the children to decide on the route they would take to a well-known local shop. Discuss how many different routes have been used. How can we decide which is the best route – the shortest, the safest, the prettiest? Ask the children to describe their routes orally (without using their hands!) and in writing. Encourage the use of left, right, forward as basic instructions. These can be related to the LOGO commands on the microcomputer and plotted using 'Turtle graphics'.

Develop the idea to allow only the use of the points of the compass, and some increasingly accurate indications of distances. The routes can be measured on the ground using a trundle wheel, or on the map using the scale. The approximate nature of both measurements should be discussed and stressed.
ATs 1, 8, 9, 11

■ Ask children to find routes which only use *one* command, for example only turns to the left are allowed, or which restrict the range of compass points which can be used such as 'all directions given must include the words north and east, the others being forbidden'.
ATs 9.11

■ Make a comparative study of measured distances of the ground, but along recognised roads or paths, on large scale maps, and 'as the crow flies'. Choose suitable destinations from the school to allow a variety of conditions.
ATs 1,8

■ Work on shops is likely to produce information about the sources of goods for stocking supermarket or small shop shelves. Particular examples of long-haul deliveries from wholesalers or major ports may be kippers, exotic fruits and electrical goods. The likely routes for delivery of such items to the shop can be investigated mathematically using road atlases.
ATs 9, 11, 12, 13

■ Use British Rail timetables to plan a journey which would last for a specified time. This is a particularly useful exercise to develop familiarity with the 24 hour clock times.
ATs 1, 8

■ The pricing policy of British Rail can be a source of investigation if planning a hypothetical or actual trip. The chosen day, time, and place can considerably alter the total cost, by taking place on different days, and with or without the use of railcards.
ATs 1, 2, 3, 4, 8

■ Use an AA, RAC or Road Atlas mileage chart to:

1 learn how to read such a chart;
2 calculate mileage, or the distance in kilometres, from the nearest large city to other interesting cities.

It is worth noting that one kilometre is approximately equal to five-eighths of a mile. Further activity can be generated from the fact that all British road signs show distances in miles only.
ATs 1, 2, 3, 4, 8

- Choose a tourist town and plan an interesting route to see a number of major attractions. Such towns are able to supply guides and maps free of charge. The route can be shown on a plan or as a sequence of instructions (with distances) and likely times of arrival and departure. The activity is made more worthwhile if an actual visit is included to 'test' the theoretical journey or itinerary.

  ATs 1, 2, 8, 9, 11

- The AA Handbook provides an excellent set of diagrams of the motorway system showing all its junctions. When used in conjunction with small scale maps more specific instructions of distances, exit numbers, and road numbers can be included in hypothetical or real journeys.

  ATs 9,11

Rubbish

- Make a collection of litter in the school playground, a local shopping precinct, or a children's playground. Rubber or plastic gloves must be worn! Tally, chart and graph the results of the collection under types of litter, for example cans, bottles, crisp bags, sweet papers, cigarette packets. Discuss relative amounts and possible reasons for them.

  ATs 9, 12, 13

School

- List the names of the people who work in the school. Sort them into sets, for example teachers, welfare assistants, secretarial staff, caretaking/cleaning staff, children. Illustrate using diagrams.
  ATs 9, 12, 13

- Find or develop timetables for the classes in the school. Compare graphically the ways time is used in the various classes and how they change depending on the age of the children.
  ATs 9, 12, 13

- Design a rota so that every child has use of a computer in a given period of time, possibly a day, a week or a month.
  ATs 9, 12, 13

- Over a period of time, survey and record the number and 'type' of visitors who come to the school, for example the nurse, LEA advisers, parents etc. Survey the purpose of the visits, using a simple questionnaire with a restricted number of alternative reasons decided in advance by the children.
  ATs 9, 12, 13

- Make a floor/room plan of the school building. Use a simple scale. Label the rooms and the various entry and exit places.
  ATs 1, 8, 9, 11

- Plan a small garden for the school. Restrict the number of aspects which must be included to, for example, two flower beds, a certain area of lawn, a path, a small vegetable patch. Vote on the best design and if possible actually build the garden – or at the very least make models for the classroom of the best designs. A great deal of measurement and mathematical decision making is required. The activity can be extended in a variety of ways, including accurate costing and considered choices of materials, seeds and the like.
  ATs 1, 3, 4, 8, 9, 12, 13

- Investigate and draw shortest routes, perhaps measured in strides to allow discussion of the approximate nature of measurement, from one part of the building to another, initially using directions based on 'left' and 'right' leading to the use of the compass and its cardinal points.
  ATs 1, 8, 9, 11

- List and analyse the durations of the school terms. If the data is available from the school office, chart differences over the last few years to take account of problems of weekends, early or late Easter, the advent of 'Baker Days' and so on.
  ATs 1,8

- Survey the numbers of wild birds seen in the school playground. Initially restrict the range to the more common birds, for example sparrow, starling, thrush, robin, blackbird, magpie, pigeon. A related activity would be to make a feeding table and make a more systematic observation over a long period.
  ATs 9, 12, 13

- Wild birds are often seen in different habitats in the school environment. Develop the survey to record relative numbers and types seen in, for example, bushes, on concrete or tarmac areas, on grass, on soil, and in high trees. Examine and record which species are seen only in one habitat. A plan of the school can be used to record the sightings. These can then be located on a form of grid reference agreed by the children.
  ATs 9, 12, 13

- Charts can be made of the feeding habits of local bird life by observing and recording behaviour:

	Worms	Insects	Snails
Thrush			
Blackbird			
Robin			
Pigeon			

Other characteristics can be recorded in a similar way, for example kinds of material used for nest building. Ideally the data should come from direct observation, but it can be supplemented by use of reference texts.
ATs 9, 12, 13

- If the person agrees, a good deal of data can be collected about the routine of, for example, the school secretary. One or two children can record the activities of the person over a period of three hours. Use of a suitable recording device is essential, for example a time chart listing one minute intervals between 9.00 a.m. and 12 noon. The approximate durations of different events are recorded and labelled with the nature of the activity. The data can then be sub-divided into categories such as typing, filing, telephone calls, counting money etc., and graphed accordingly.
  ATs 1, 5, 9, 12, 13

- The school registers can be a major source of simple statistics about the children of a school. The registers, and the admissions books if available, can be used to analyse the recent 'history' of the school statistically. The numbers of boys and girls in each age group, total class numbers, the incidence and patterns of absence, the incidence of 'family' names are all available in an easy to read and count form. It is, however, important to ensure that any personal and confidential matters are deleted before allowing children to use such documents.
  ATs 1, 3, 5, 9, 12, 13

Shelves

■ Members of the class can design and build a shelf, or set of shelves, for a small classroom library. The same mathematical decisions have to be made as in a full size school or town library:

Locating the shelf, which wall, height, depth of shelves;
Free-standing or wall-fixed;
Design, solid or slatted, number of shelves, sidewall or brackets;
Cost;
Order of work, including range and quantity of equipment required;
Allocation of duties among the building team.

Finally actually building the shelves to give a point to the exercise.
ATs 1, 2, 3, 4, 8

Shops

■ List the kinds of shops available in a local 'parade' or small precinct. Make a list of the sorts of items which can be purchased in each of the shops. Which shop sells the largest range of items?
ATs 9, 12, 13

- It is likely that some items can be purchased at more than one shop. Record the occurrence of common and specific items using Venn or Carroll diagrams, or a simple arrow diagram.
  ATs 9, 12, 13

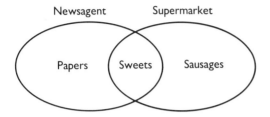

- Discuss which of the businesses are not really 'shops'. Some, such as building societies, banks, solicitors' offices, or a dry-cleaning business may look like shops but provide a service rather than selling things. One or two will provide a service and sell goods (such as a sub-post office). This sort of data can be recorded using Venn or Carroll diagrams.
  ATs 9, 12, 13

	Selling goods	Not selling goods
Providing a service	Post Office	Bank
Not providing a service	Supermarket	Closed-down premises(?)

- Survey and compare the type and range of shops to be found in different locations, for example a small corner shop, a city centre precinct, a suburban shopping parade.
  ATs 9, 12, 13

- Survey the shopping habits of a sample of people who pass the school gates, or who are in a 'safe' environment to be interviewed. The size of the sample needs to be decided upon and a suitable range of questions chosen to elicit data capable of analysis. Asking which people buy items in supermarkets or small shops, or both will produce data suitable for recording on Venn or Carroll diagrams. Reasons may be requested, for example price, locality, range/selection available, and can be analysed in tabular form. Children will find that interesting answers about shopping habits will arise from including interviews with men who are shopping!
  ATs 1, 8, 9, 12, 13

- Most shopping precincts have a 'map' of the shops which are available. A copy of the plan can be completed using a colour coding system for 'types' of shops or businesses to show a pattern of provision. Discuss the type of shops that are not available in the precinct and the types that children would like to see.
  ATs 1, 3, 8, 9, 12

- Using a local supermarket as the source, list the major departments of the shop, for example household goods, 'produce' (fruit and vegetables), grocery, meat, bakery, frozen goods and dairy produce. Record the range of items available using arrow diagrams.
  ATs 9, 12

- Most major supermarkets try to design the location of shelves and sections to make shopping easier. Discuss and plan:

  1 shopping lists to take account of the current layout of the supermarket;
  2 possible changes in the layout of a shop to improve ease of shopping for children in primary age groups.
  ATs 1, 8, 9, 12, 13

74

- Survey the numbers of customers who visit shops of various sizes at different times of the day. Tally and record using a suitable means. It is worth noting that most major supermarket chains possess their own research data about this which could be compared with the small scale survey undertaken.
  ATs 9, 12, 13

- Interview the managers of shops of different sizes to determine the number of staff who work there. The data can be subdivided into types of job: part-time and full-time, male and female.
  ATs 9, 12, 13

- Given a map or plan of a group of available shops get children to design a route which would most efficiently complete a shopping list, for example bulky or heavy items should be purchased last. Encourage the children to design shopping lists which group together the required items to increase the ease of shopping.
  ATs 9, 12, 13

- List the sorts of items the children would regard as essential in a small village shop. This can be decided on the basis of an 'essentials' and 'luxuries' subdivision of a list suggested by the children themselves.
  ATs 9, 12, 13

- A visit to a local branch of a large chain of shops provides an opportunity for children to see at first hand the operation of a modern cashtill and its means of recording transactions. Many of the larger chains make use of computerised stock systems based on the increasingly familiar bar codes. These are worthy of informal investigation at the primary stage before more formal work on Information Technology in secondary education. General points of procedure such as till receipt codes and bar codes can be investigated.
  ATs 1, 2, 3, 4, 8

- Very useful data can be produced from interviews with elderly people who often have remarkable recall of prices in earlier decades. This can lead to work on pre-decimal currency as a curiosity, and some examination of the concept of price inflation.
  ATs 1, 2, 3, 4, 8

- Many shopping precincts have lifts. Examine the weight limit and/or limit of the number of people who can be carried at one time. Discuss possible body weights, and numbers of members of the class who could safely travel in a lift without exceeding the limit.
  ATs 1, 2, 3, 4, 8

Signs and signals

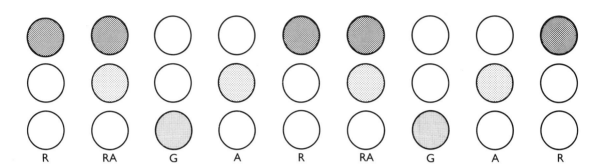

R　RA　G　A　R　RA　G　A　R

■ Examine the sequence of traffic lights. They can initially be recorded as a series of diagrams, then as a series of words, and finally as a series of symbols, perhaps to form a mnemonic such as **R-RAGAR**.
ATs 1, 5

■ Collect examples of notices for jumble sales, and theatre/cinema performances which have been posted in shops or the library. Analyse them to determine times, costs, possible duration, dates. Get the children to design and produce the posters for a forthcoming school function.
ATs 1, 2, 3, 4, 8

■ Using a listing of road signs, analyse each one for regular and non-regular shapes, or for symmetry.
ATs 9, 10, 11

■ Road signs indicating hills can be a rich source of mathematics, and gradients can be written as fractions, ratios, decimals and percentages. Make models of some of the observed gradients and experiment by rolling cars, to determine distances travelled 'without a push'.
ATs 1, 3, 5, 8

Steep hill
downwards

Steep hill
upwards

Sports and games

Use newspaper and magazine pictures of horse races and/or people running in athletics meetings to reinforce the important concepts of ordinal numbers, i.e. first, second and third. This is used naturally in team and individual games in school sports, but can be discussed 'mathematically' using a picture form of representation. Cards printed with positions can be used as a mathematical motivating device for rapid changing of clothes after PE lessons!

ATs 1, 2, 3, 4

Investigate the design of a running track, developing the idea of the need for staggered starts by investigating, if possible, a real track and tracing the length of each lane. This could also be investigated in the classroom using, first, a set of concentric circles and then the normal track with two 'straights' and the connecting 'bends'.

ATs 9, 10, 11

Investigate the design of the throwing sector in major competitions, including the use of the net to catch any wayward throws which might injure spectators.

ATs 1, 8, 9, 10, 11

Cycling is a common sport or hobby. The structure of a variety of bicycle frames can be examined using straws, geostrips or similar. The need for rigidity can be examined if children attempt to design their own 'new' bicycle frame.

ATs 9, 10, 11

Heart beats and/or pulse rates can be measured before and after exercise. This can be included in a whole series of investigations of lung capacity, physical endurance (such as holding out arms horizontally) and strength.

ATs 1, 2, 3, 8

77

- Investigate the distance-time graphs which produce a parabola when, for example, a ball is thrown into the air, or a diver leaves a platform. Particularly useful in this respect is the computer program 'Mangonel'.
  ATS 1, 3, 5, 7

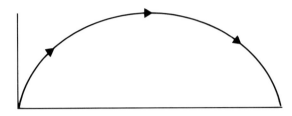

- Sports times and records can be recorded from major international competitions. Questions of accuracy of measurement and timing are raised. World records can be compared with those of the children in the class.
  ATs 1, 8

- Sports fields, pitches and courts can be measured and scale drawings made.
  ATs 1, 8

- On a football field the available angle for a shot at goal to be made varies with the position of the player. Investigate sound positions from which to take shots, and the related expected position of the goalkeeper.
  ATs 9, 11

- Sailing races on an international level are common. Investigate the distances involved, the concept of a 'knot' as a nautical measure, and introduce the concept of 'bearings' in this context.
  ATs 1, 8, 9, 11

- Orienteering is a growing sport to which many teachers belong, particularly in secondary schools. A talk from an active participant generates interest in map reading, particularly the understanding of contours symbols and the reading of coordinates and scale distances. A small scale version of the sport can be designed as a 'treasure hunt' in the school, its environment or in the local park. It is a particularly useful activity for the development of the concept of 'bearings'.
  ATs 1, 8, 9, 11

- Use local or national league tables to examine positions and changes over time. Analyse the columns of the table: games played – won – drawn – lost – goals for – goals against – points.
  ATs 9, 12, 13

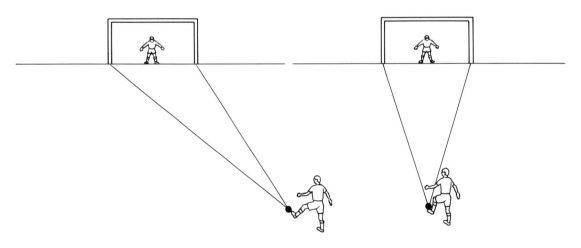

- The local swimming pool usually has a timetable of availability. Survey and analyse the times allocated to:
  ATs 9, 12, 13

	Times	Total hours
Adult non-swimmers		
Infant learners		
Clubs		
Family sessions etc		

- The leisure or sports centre usually has a list of charges for a wide range of activities and age groups. Examine the costs of the whole class using the centre for a particular range of activities. Is it cheaper to pay separately or to book the whole range of activities as a block booking?
  ATs 1, 2, 3, 4, 8

- The common sport of fishing can generate a good deal of mathematical investigation of, for example, sorting types of fish, breaking points of different types of line and locations of suitable places to fish.
  ATs 9, 12, 13

- Score cards and scoring books for games such as golf and cricket can be a source of data for analysis. In golf the ideas of 'par', 'birdies' and 'eagles', and handicaps can be fruitful. In cricket the particular arrangement of the score book to define overs, extras etc., can be examined, as can the scoring system for county games and the well-developed idea of bowling and batting averages.
  ATs 1, 2, 3, 4, 8

The street

- List and graph the numbers of children who live in roads named '? Street', '? Avenue', '? Road'.
  ATs 9, 12, 13

- Pick a local street. Survey the kinds of buildings found there, for example houses, bungalows, small shops, offices. Sort and record on a graph.
  ATs 9, 12, 13

- Introduce the four points of the compass, decide upon and discuss the direction of the major streets lived in by the class.
  ATs 1, 8, 9, 11

- Describe in writing the route taken by children to reach school, ensuring correct use of 'left' and 'right' etc.
  ATs 9, 11

- Examine the sequence of traffic lights. They can be described using a series of diagrams. The idea of a cyclical sequence can be introduced and related to the time cycle of day-night-day, etc.
  ATs 1, 8, 9, 11

- Make a simple map of a route from the school to another local building. The distance can be measured using a trundle wheel or a stop clock to record the time taken (under supervision).
  ATs 1, 8

- On a simple plan of a child's street, record the house numbers. Discuss the fact that, normally, the even numbers are on one side and the odd numbers on the other. Such aspects as the numbers of houses between numbers 3 and 11 can be investigated.
  ATs 1, 2, 3, 5

- Set up a series of puzzle journeys, for example 'I leave the school gate and turn left, I turn first right and stop at the second house on the left. Where am I?'
  ATs 9, 11

- Imagine that an important visitor is coming to the school. Decide on and describe, with approximate measurements or landmarks indicated, a route to get to the school from the railway station, bus stop, or local hotel.
  ATs 1, 8, 9, 11

- Look for and list the 'solid' shapes found in the environment, in particular the cylinder, cube, cuboid and triangular prism. These can be matched and compared with the classroom set of 'solid shapes'.
  ATs 9, 10

- Make a list of fixed objects normally found in a street, for example telephone boxes, post boxes, lamp posts etc. Count, tally and record the information using mappings, arrow diagrams or a block graph.
  ATs 9, 10, 11, 12, 13

- Survey, tally and record the numbers of vehicles using a street, for example cars, buses, lorries, vans, bicycles. This can be repeated at different times of the day or on different days to try to establish patterns of behaviour in the children's environment.
  ATs 9, 12, 13

- Survey and record the reasons why a given number of people are in the street at a given time. Sort the information according to a simple set of sub-divisions, for example shopping, working, going to work, or merely taking a walk.
  ATs 9, 12, 13

- Find and copy tessellating patterns in the street, for example paving stones, brickwork, scaffolding.
  ATs 9, 10, 11

- Take rubbings of interesting designs of grids, manhole covers, etc. Similarly, different textures of brick, paving, or doors can be 'rubbed' or copied, or photographs can be taken. They can be discussed in the classroom and their 'mathematical' characteristics analysed.
  ATs 9, 10, 11

Pillar box   Cylinder   Roof   Triangular prism

- In a local car park, measure the size of the bays using a standard, but arbitrary, measuring device. Using the same device compare this with the width of a car.
  ATs 1, 8

- Survey and record the different makes, colours, ages and types of vehicles in a small car park. Compare the results with the cars found in the staff car park.
  ATs 9, 12, 13

- Survey the different street signs found in a street or main road. Use the Highway Code to determine the meaning of the signs. Discuss signs that the children in the class might like to see. Design and draw, in colour, such a sign. Get the children to write to the Borough Council proposing that their sign be used. It can elicit some interesting replies!
  ATs 1, 5, 9, 11

- Survey and find the meaning of the highway markings, for example double yellow lines, found in the street.
  ATs 9, 10, 11

- Parking restrictions can be a good source of 'time' topics, for example 'Waiting time limited to 20 minutes. No return within two hours'. Ask children: 'How many times would your mum have to move her car in a day at the shops?'
  'ATs 1, 2, 3, 4, 8

Toys

- List and sort the favourite toys owned by the class. They can be sorted according to type, colour, size, function and so on.
  ATs 9, 12, 13

- Using a selection of available comics, discuss and produce a chart of relative popularity. Discuss reasons for choices. These can be grouped and charted, for example use of colour, TV characters included, contain puzzles etc.
  ATs 9, 12, 13

- Survey and record the amounts of money spent on comics by members of the class. Calculate the total cost of a year's supply of one, or more comics.
  ATs 1, 2, 3, 4, 9, 12, 13

- Each comic has an issue number. Assuming there are 52 issues in each year, find the date when the first issue was produced. This is a particularly interesting exercise with long-established comics such as *Dandy* and *Beano*.
  ATs 1, 2, 3, 4

- Calculate an average child's total pocket money for one year. How many issues of a single comic could be bought? Could the child afford to buy a comic every day?
  ATs 1, 2, 3, 4

- Ask a newsagent how many copies of a particular comic are purchased from the wholesaler as a standard order. Calculate the amount of money taken on the one comic.
  ATs 1, 2, 3, 4

- Ask a newsagent to say how much profit she/he makes on particular comics. Calculate this as a fraction, decimal or percentage of the total cost.
  ATs 1, 2, 3, 4

- Design a 'new' front page for a comic, including space for the border, the number of 'boxes' to be used and the amount of space for the heading or title. Invent a title and calculate ways to centre it on the page.
  ATs 9, 10, 11

- Survey favourite comic or cartoon characters and record opinions in a suitable form.
  ATs 9, 12, 13

- Make a mobile of the solid shapes currently being learned by the class. These are likely to include the cube, cuboid, cylinder, and assorted prisms. The mobiles can be balanced in a symmetrical way or simply labelled to provide a classroom reminder of names of solids.
  ATs 9, 10

- Use old cardboard boxes, or sealed shoe boxes, to construct a robot figure of whatever height desired. If the season is right, a large Father Christmas can be made in this way. The mathematics arises from the need to get the proportions correct.
  ATs 9, 10

- Investigate what would be the ideal length for a skipping rope for an individual, a small group, or for the whole class. It would involve trying out ropes of different lengths to see which was most efficient for each child. This could be measured by the number of skips a child could manage to do in a given time. The lengths could be measured using arbitrary units or by direct comparison, one with another.
  ATs 1, 8

- Introduce or develop the idea of 'circumference' by rolling a bicycle wheel, starting and ending on a mark made on the tyre. This can be related to the radius of the wheel to give a real-world application of the ratio.
  ATs 1, 8

Water

Each person uses on average about 150 litres of water each day. This is roughly divided into 40 litres for lavatory flushing, 35 litres for washing and bathing, 25 litres for drinking and cooking, 20 litres for washing clothes, 15 litres for washing dishes, and 15 litres for use on such activities as watering gardens, washing cars and filling the pond.

This data can be used to measure and record the normal consumption of families of different sizes, and the amounts used by the families in the class in a week, a month, and a year. The consumption for the town in which the school is situated can be calculated. The subdivision of the data can be used to highlight the use of percentages.

ATs 1, 8

A good activity to reinforce the concept of area is to investigate the surface area of the pre-cast plastic ponds on display at most large garden centres. There can be two aspects to the investigation:

1 Measurement of the surface area of the water it contains when full. This can be measured using a grid of metre, half-metre or decimetre squares made from string. This is held over the surface and the approximate number of squares counted using the standard 'area of irregular shapes' method.
2 The internal surface area of the plastic used for the pond can be found by using the same grid, which is dropped into the space and which follows the 'contours' of the shape.

In both cases the points where the grid touches the edges of the pond can be marked using felt tip pens or small loops of sticky tape.

ATs 1, 8

Bibliography

BOLT, B. (1985) *Mathematical Activities*. Cambridge University Press.

BOLT, B. (1985) *More Mathematical Activities*. Cambridge University Press.

BOLT, B. (1987) *Even More Mathematical Activities*. Cambridge University Press.

BURTON, L. (1984) *Thinking Things Through*. Blackwell.

CHARLES, R. (1985) *Problem Solving Experiences in Mathematics*. Addison Wesley.

CUNDY, H. M. and ROLLETT, A. P. (1987) *Mathematical Models*. Tarquin.

DENYER, J. (1983) *Mathematics Across The Curriculum*. SCDC.

DEPARTMENT OF EDUCATION AND SCIENCE (1985) *Mathematics 5–16*. HMSO.

DEPARTMENT OF EDUCATION AND SCIENCE (1985) *The Curriculum from 5 to 16*. HMSO.

DEPARTMENT OF EDUCATION AND SCIENCE (1989) *National Curriculum: From Policy to Practice*. HMSO.

DEPARTMENT OF EDUCATION AND SCIENCE (1989) *Mathematics: Non-Statutory Guidance to the National Curriculum*. HMSO.

DEPARTMENT OF EDUCATION AND SCIENCE (1989) *Science: Non-Statutory Guidance to the National Curriculum*. HMSO.

DIAGRAM GROUP (1982) *The Book Of Comparisons*. Penguin.

FISHER, R. (ed.) (1987) *Problem Solving in Primary Schools*. Blackwell.

GOLDWATER, D. (1975) *Bridges and How They Are Built*. World's Work.

HARBIN, R. (1980) *Teach Yourself Origami*. Hodder and Stoughton.

HARLING, P. (1990) *Cambridge Primary Maths: Skill Support Activities (Set 2)*. Cambridge University Press.

HARLING, P. (1988) *Maths Plus*, Books 1 to 27 and the Teacher's Resource Book. Ward Lock Educational.

HARLING, P. (1989) *Calculated To Please: Calculator Activities For The National Curriculum*, Books 1 to 3. Unwin Hyman.

HARLING, P. and ROBERTS, T. (1988) *Primary Mathematics Schemes: How To Choose and Use*. Hodder and Stoughton.

HOGBEN, L. (1989) *Mathematics For The Million*. Pan.

HOGBEN, L. (1968) *Man Must Measure*. Rathbone.

HOLLANDS, R. (1986) *Let's Solve Problems*. Blackwell.

JOHNSEY, R. (1986) *Problem Solving in School Science*. Macdonald.

LANCASHIRE COUNTY COUNCIL (1986) *The Lancaster Project For The Able Child In The Primary School*. Lancashire County Council.

LEAPFROGS (1977) *Codes*. Tarquin.

MANCHESTER EDUCATION COMMITTEE (1986) *Problem Solving in Science and Technology*.

MASON, J., BURTON, L. and STACEY, K. (1982) *Thinking Mathematically*. Addison Wesley.

MEYER, C. and SALEE, T. (1983) *Make it Simpler: A Practical Guide to Problem Solving in Mathematics*. Addison Wesley.

MINISTRY OF TRANSPORT (1988) *The Highway Code*. HMSO.

MOTTERSHEAD, L. (1985) *Investigations in Mathematics*. Blackwell.

MOTTERSHEAD, L. (1978) *Sources of Mathematical Discovery*. Blackwell.

NATIONAL CURRICULUM COUNCIL (1988) *English in the National Curriculum*. HMSO.

NATIONAL CURRICULUM COUNCIL (1988) *Mathematics in the National Curriculum*. HMSO.

NATIONAL CURRICULUM COUNCIL (1988) *Science in the National Curriculum*. HMSO.

OPEN UNIVERSITY (PME 233) (1980) *Mathematics Across The Curriculum*. Open University Press.

RICHARDS, C. and HOLFORD, D. (eds.) (1985) *The Teaching of Primary Science: Policy and Practice.* Falmer Press.

SCHOOLS COUNCIL (1972) *Mathematics For The Majority Project; Crossing Subject Boundaries.* Chatto and Windus.

SCHOOLS COUNCIL (1976) *Place, Time and Society 8–13.* SCDC.

SHOOTER, K. and SAXTON, J. (1988) *Making Things Work.* Cambridge University Press.

SMITH, T. (1972) *The Story of Measurement.* Blackwell.

SPODE GROUP (1981) *Solving Real Problems with Mathematics.* Cranfield Press.

STOKER, A. (ed.) (1986) *Problem Solving in Primary Schools.* Sunderland SATRO.

TUMA, D. T. and REIF, F. (1980) *Problem Solving and Education.* Lawrence Erlbaum.

WHITTAKER, D. (1986) *Will Gulliver's Suit Fit? Mathematical Problem Solving with Children.* Cambridge University Press.

Index